ADULT GUIDE TO CHILDREN'S TEAM SPORTS

ADULT GUIDE TO CHILDREN'S TEAM SPORTS

JAMES H. HUMPHREY
DEBORAH A. YOW

WITHDRAWN

Nova Science Publishers, Inc.
New York

Senior Editors: Susan Boriotti and Donna Dennis
Coordinating Editor: Tatiana Shohov
Office Manager: Annette Hellinger
Graphics: Wanda Serrano
Editorial Production: Jennifer Vogt, Matthew Kozlowski, Jonathan Rose
and Maya Columbus
Circulation: Ave Maria Gonzalez, Raymond Davis and Vladimir Klestov
Communications and Acquisitions: Serge P. Shohov
Marketing: Cathy DeGregory

Library of Congress Cataloging-in-Publication Data
Available Upon Request

ISBN: 1-59033-317-9

Copyright © 2002 by Nova Science Publishers, Inc.
400 Oser Ave, Suite 1600
Hauppauge, New York 11788-3619
Tel: 631-231-7269   Fax 631-231-8175
e-mail: Novascience@earthlink.net
Web Site: http://www.novapublishers.com

All rights reserved. No part of this book may be reproduced, stored in a retrieval system or
transmitted in any form or by any means: electronic, electrostatic, magnetic, tape, mechanical
photocopying, recording or otherwise without permission from the publishers.

The authors and publisher have taken care in preparation of this book, but make no expressed
or implied warranty of any kind and assume no responsibility for any errors or omissions. No
liability is assumed for incidental or consequential damages in connection with or arising out of
information contained in this book.

This publication is designed to provide accurate and authoritative information with regard to
the subject matter covered herein. It is sold with the clear understanding that the publisher is
not engaged in rendering legal or any other professional services. If legal or any other expert
assistance is required, the services of a competent person should be sought. FROM A
DECLARATION OF PARTICIPANTS JOINTLY ADOPTED BY A COMMITTEE OF THE
AMERICAN BAR ASSOCIATION AND A COMMITTEE OF PUBLISHERS.

Printed in the United States of America

CONTENTS

ABOUT THE AUTHORS

James H. Humphrey, Professor Emeritus of the University of Maryland, is the author or co-author of 52 books, several of which are about childhood fitness and physical education. His articles and research reports have appeared in more than 20 national and international journals and magazines.

Deborah A. Yow is a strong advocate for children's sports, and has received numerous national awards for excellence in sports administration. She is the author, co-author and contributing author of 12 books and is author of numerous articles in prestigious periodicals. She is a frequent speaker at workshops, seminars and meetings of educators and athletic administrators. She has collaborated with Dr. Humphrey on two books and several articles concerned with various aspects of sports.

LIST OF FIGURES

INTRODUCTION

We will first provide some working definitions for certain terms used in the title of the book. The term *team sports* is used to mean *organized interactions of children in competitive and/or cooperative team physical activities*. The term *children* includes those boys and girls through the chronological age of 12 (ordinarily the final year of elementary school). For purposes here *adults* are the child overseers (parents, teachers, coaches, and others) who are currently involved, or plan to become involved in some way in children's sports.

The growth of children's sports has reached almost unbelievable proportions. Using Little League Baseball as an example, there are around 3 million participants on almost 200,000 teams in more than 60 countries. In addition, more than 750,000 volunteers world-wide participate in this program.

As mentioned previously, the highest age level considered here is one reached by most children in the last year of elementary school (6th grade). Children's sports, as conceived here, are not a prominent part of many elementary school programs. There are some instances where elementary schools support interscholastic or varsity sports programs, but for the most part this is not the norm. On the other hand, the major emphasis is placed on a well-balanced physical education program where all children have an equal opportunity to participate. However, some elementary schools provide sports programs in the form of *intramural* activities. This is a natural outgrowth of the physical education program with teams organized so that one classroom may play against another. This usually occurs after school and is supervised by school officials.

The great preponderance of children's sports programs take place outside of school and are not ordinarily conducted under the supervision of the school. They are usually sponsored by such organizations as recreation centers, business enterprises, and assorted boys' and girls' clubs.

Over the years such organizations as Little League Baseball, Midget Football, Pop Warner Football, Itty Bitty Basketball, Pee Wee Golf along with a host of others have flourished and attracted children in amazingly large numbers, which some estimates place well in excess of 40 million.

Contrary to general belief, sports experience for children is not of recent origin. In fact, educators and philosophers as far back as the early Greeks felt that sports-oriented activities might be a welcome adjunct to the total education of children. For instance, over 2,300 years ago Plato suggested that all early education should be a sort of play and should develop around play situations.

In the 17th century, Locke, the English philosopher, felt that children should get plenty of exercise and learn to swim early in life. Rousseau, the notable French writer, held much the same opinion, believing that learning should develop from the enjoyable physical activities of childhood. These men, along with numerous others, influenced to some extent the path that children's sports was to follow through ensuing decades.

There have been periods in our history when any type of sports program was abandoned purely on the basis that body pleasure of any type must be subjugated because this activity was associated with a foolish or unnecessary expenditure of time and energy or even evil doing. The early American pioneers more or less typified this kind of puritanical thinking because there was little or no emphasis on sports for the pioneer child, certainly organized team sports. In addition to this rationale was also the absence of free time and available sports equipment as we know it today.

Eventually, however, attitudes changed and interest in children's sports began to emerge. Instrumental in the movement was the establishment of the first public playground in Boston in 1885. This idea soon spread nationwide with children from one playground competing in various sports activities with those from other playgrounds.

It was not long before enterprising merchants saw possibilities for advertising by sponsoring various teams, thus capitalizing by organizing the traditional neighborhood games of children. It certainly made any child proud to be wearing a shirt with "Sherman's Grocery" or Morton's Drugstore" emblazoned on the back.

In more modern times a much different outlook has characterized the area of children's sports. And much of this involves the *physical fitness* of children. In fact, over a period of several decades there have been varying degrees of interest in the physical fitness of children and youth. In the early 1950s the publication of the results of six physical fitness tests (named after the authors – Kraus-Webber Tests) stimulated a great deal of concern about the physical fitness of American children. These tests had been conducted with large numbers of European children and comparisons made with the results of the tests administered to a sample of children in Westchester County, New York. The fact that this geographical area at the time was considered to be one of the country's highest socioeconomic levels made the results of this comparison all the more appalling to the citizens of the United States.

The validity and reliability of these tests, as well as the conditions under which they were administered, tended to arouse criticism among some of the skeptics of that time. Nonetheless the results did serve the purpose of alerting American educators and laymen alike to the alleged physical status of the nation's children.

As a result, then President Eisenhower appointed Shane McCarthy, a Washington, DC lawyer, to head a committee on Fitness of American Children and Youth. Among others, this committee consisted of assorted professional boxers and a famous racehorse trainer. While the intentions of these individuals were not necessarily questioned, at the same time their knowledge and understanding of childhood fitness was of concern to many. And since that time the various Chairmen of the President's Council on Physical Fitness and Sports have been appointed mainly because of their public name-recognition rather than their knowledge of fitness of children.

Since its early emphasis, childhood fitness through sports has experienced various degrees of success. Interest has continued to a point that now children's sports are enjoying almost unprecedented support, development and enthusiasm.

The authors' combined experience in children's sports as participant, observer, parent, teacher, or coach spans upwards of eight decades. At the outset we want to make it luminously clear that it is *not* the purpose of this book to extol or criticize the area of children's sports. On the contrary, we want to present the facts – pro and con – as we understand them with the reader coming to his or her own conclusions.

In the introductory chapter a general overview of team sports for children presents such issues and background information as competition, injuries, and supervision as well as the more negative aspects. Chapter 2 deals with the formulation of a philosophy and objectives for children's sports. In Chapter 3 there is a discussion of the various elements involved in the basic sports skills needed for successful participation. Chapters 4-8 are devoted to a discussion of what extensive studies show are the most popular team sports for children. Included in these chapters are explanations of various sports skills that need to be achieved for success. A distinguishing feature in these chapters is the many games that can be used to practice the various sports skills. The final chapter takes into account the knowledge that adults should have in order to make a scientific approach in teaching children about sports skills.

Most books are the result of author exchange with other people. This volume is no exception. Along with our own personal experience in this area, we have consulted with both proponents and critics of children's sports, which included parents, professional athletes, children's coaches, school personnel, and children themselves. (With regard to the latter, we are particularly grateful to the hundreds of children who responded to the *Humphrey Sports Inventory for Children*.) We have tried to merge all of this information into what we hope will be a sensible guide for those adults – coaches, parents, and others – who are involved in, or plan to be involved in, children's sports in a way that will always be in the best interest of the child.

Chapter 1

IMPORTANT BACKGROUND INFORMATION FOR ADULTS

There are a number of factors that adults should be concerned with when they become involved in children's sports. In this regard, the issues dealt with in this chapter are competition, injuries, supervision, and unfortunately the negative side of children's sports.

COMPETITION

The positive and negative aspects of sports competition for children have been debated for decades. In fact, over 40 years ago the first author was the chairman of a national committee on "Competition for Children." After studying the matter with some degree of thoroughness, the "experts" on the committee decided that the success or failure of such competition was dependent upon the type of supervision provided for overseeing such programs. (Supervision of children's sports will be discussed later in the chapter.)

There has always been a concern for the emotional stress that competition can have on a child. And, of course, such emotional stress can impact on a child's physical well-being. In fact, a new policy from the American Academy of Pediatricians states that children should be discouraged from specializing in a single sport before adolescence to avoid physical and psychological negative effects.

In a study conducted with 200 5th and 6th grade children, one of the questions asked was "What is the one thing that *worries* you most in school?" As might be expected there were a variety of responses. However, the one general characteristic that tended to emerge was the emphasis placed on competition in so many school situations. Although students did not state this specifically, the nature of their responses clearly indicated this sentiment.

Most of the literature on competition for children has focused on sports activities. However, there are many situations that exist in some classrooms that can cause competitive stress. An example is the antiquated "Spelling Bee" which still exists in some schools, and in fact, continues to be recognized in an annual national competition. Perhaps the first few children "spelled down" are likely to be the ones who need spelling practice the most. And, to say the least, it can be humiliating and embarrassing in front of others to fail in any school task.

It is interesting to note that the terms *cooperation* and *competition* are antonymous. Therefore, the reconciliation of children's competitive needs and cooperative needs is not an easy matter. In a sense, we are confronted with an ambivalent condition which, if not carefully handled, could place children in a state of conflict, thus causing them to endure distress.

This was recognized by Horney[1] over half a century ago when she indicated that we must not only be assertive but aggressive, able to push others out of the way. On the other hand, we are deeply imbued with ideals which declare that it is selfish to want anything for ourselves, thus we should be humble, turn the other hand, be yielding. Accordingly, society not only rewards one kind of behavior (cooperation) but also its direct opposite (competition). Perhaps more often than not our cultural demands sanction these rewards without provision of clear-cut standards of value with regard to specific conditions under which these forms of behavior might well be practiced. Thus, the child is sometimes placed in a quandary as to when to compete and when to cooperate.

It has also been found that competition does not necessarily lead to peak performance, and may in fact interfere with achievement. In this connection, Kohn[2] reported on a survey on the effects of competition in sports, business, and classroom achievement and found that 65 studies showed that cooperation promoted higher achievement than competition, 8 showed the reverse, and 36 showed no statistically significant differences. It was concluded that the trouble with competition is that it makes one person's success depend on another's failure, and as a result when success depends on sharing resources, competition can get in the way and therefore inhibit the process.

In studying about competitive stress Scanlan and Passer[3] described this condition as occurring when a child feels (perceives) that he or she will not be able to perform adequately to the performance demands of competition. When the child feels this way, he or she experiences considerable threat to self-esteem which results in stress. They also described competitive stress as the negative emotion or anxiety that a child experiences when he or she perceived the competition to be personally threatening. Indeed, this is a condition that should not be allowed to prevail in any environment – school or out-of-school.

Studying the problem objectively, Scanlan[4] used a sports environment to identify predictors of competitive stress. She investigated the influence and stability of individual differences and situational factors on the competitive stress experienced by 76 9-to-14-year-old wrestlers. The subjects represented 16 teams from one state and reflected a wide range of wrestling ability and experience. Stress was assessed by the children's form of the Competitive State Anxiety Inventory and was measured immediately before and after each of two consecutive tournament matches.

The children's dispositions, characteristic pre-competition cognitions, perception of significant adult influences, psychological states, self-perceptions and competitive outcomes were examined as predictors of pre- and post-match anxiety in separate multiple regression analyses for each tournament round. The most influential and stable predictors of pre-match stress for both matches were competitive stress anxiety and personal performance expectancies, while win-loss and fun experienced during the match predicted post-match stress for both rounds.

Pre-match worries about failure and perceived parental pressure to participate were predictive to Round One pre-match stress. Round One post-match stress levels predicted stress after Round Two, suggesting some consistence in the children's stress responses. Sixty-one and 35 percent pre-match and 41 percent and 32 percent of post-match state anxiety variances was explained for Rounds One and Two, respectively.

On the basis of the available evidence with regard to the subject of competition, it seems justifiable to formulate the following general concepts.

1. Very young children in general are not very competitive but become more so as they grow older.
2. There is a wide variety in competition among children; that is, some are violently competitive, while others are mildly competitive, and still others are not competitive at all.
3. Boys are more competitive than girls.
4. Competition should be adjusted so that there is not a preponderant number of highly experienced and skilled competitors teams against others who are grossly lesser in experience and ability.
5. Competition and rivalry can sometimes produce results in effort and speed of accomplishment.

Adults involved in children's sports might well be guided by the above concepts. Whether you are a proponent or critic of competitive sports for children, it has now become evident that such competition may be "here to stay." Thus, positively controlling it might be our greater concern. This might perhaps be done by concentrating our efforts in the direction of educating both adults and children regarding the positive and negative effects of competition.

INJURIES

The things that concerns parents – particularly mothers – the most about their children's participation in sports is the possibility of injury. And rightfully so, because it is estimated that upwards of one million children report to a hospital every year because of sports injuries. This could actually be much larger because many injuries are not reported. Add to this the fact that a number of such injuries are very serious or fatal. In fact, the National Youth Sports Safety Foundation reported 276 deaths from sports injuries for a 14-year period, 1984-1998.[5] Key findings of the report included: The number one cause of deaths involved trauma to the head; 45 percent of these deaths occurred in just two sporting activities; the number of deaths per year are fairly consistent at approximately 22 a year; four of the five top sports where the most deaths occurred are among the most popular sports – baseball, football, basketball, and soccer.

It should be borne in mind that contrary to popular opinion, accidents resulting in injury do not "just happen." More than 90 percent of such accidents are caused. Although injuries do occur, many of them can be avoided if proper precautions are taken. Thus, appropriate care should be taken to assure the well-being of the child participant.

Two former University of Maryland doctoral students, Robert G. Davis and Larry D. Issacs have devised the following set of guidelines for those responsible for conducting children's sports programs.

1. Use quality constructed and properly fitting protective gear.
2. Match teams for competition on the basis of physical fitness, skill level and physical maturation (biological age) – not chronological age only.
3. Children should not be forced into sport participation. Children who do not want to be involved in a sport are at high risk for injury.
4. Young participants should be encouraged to play different sports and experience different positions within a given sport. This practice tends to reduce injuries which may be a result of over-stressing a particular movement pattern.
5. Pay close attention to signs of physical fatigue. Many injuries occur late in a game or practice session when the children are tired. Unfortunately, the image conveyed by some coaches, "be tough," keeps many young athletes from telling the coach of their fatigue.

There are certain conditions traditionally associated with sports. "Tennis elbow" is a case in point. This is an inflammation of the rounded portion of the bone at the elbow joint. The name is no doubt a misnomer because the majority of these cases are a result of activities other than swinging a tennis racquet.

The same could probably be said of what has become commonly known as "Little League elbow." The technical name for this condition in *osteochondritis capitulum* which like "tennis elbow" is an inflammation of a bone and its cartilage at the elbow joint. It is caused generally by a hard and prolonged act of throwing using the overarm throwing pattern. One would not have to be a "Little Leaguer" to contract this condition. Simply playing catch and throwing hard to a partner for prolonged periods could also bring this about.

One of the most feared injuries in sports, or any activity for that matter, are those of the eyes. In this regard, Orlando[7] did an interesting study to determine the severity and frequency of soccer-related eye injuries. The medical charts of 13 soccer players who had sustained blunt trauma to the eye were reviewed. The patients (five girls, eight boys) ranged in age from 8 to 15 years. The most common injury was *hyphemia* (a hemorrhage in the eyeball). Others included *retinal edema* (excessive accumulation of fluid in the innermost layer of the eye), *secondary glaucoma* (increased pressure within the eyeball), *chorioretinal rupture* (an inflammatory condition in the back of the eye), and *angle recession*. Six injuries were caused by the soccer ball, three by a kick, and one by a head butt. In three cases the cause was unknown. As a result of the study, the author made the following recommendations: (1) education of coaching staff, parents, and officials; (2) protective eye wear; (3) proper conditioning; (4) strictly enforced rules; and (5) an emphasis on having fun to help reduce the number and severity of soccer-related eye injuries.

For more than 40 years some critics have been concerned with possible injuries that children might sustain in *contact* sports, especially football. This concern has centered around the notion that too much pressure would be applied to the *epiphyses*, particularly in such activities as football.

In the long bones there is first a center of ossification for the bone called the *diaphysis*. As each new portion is ossified thin layers of cartilage continue to develop between the diaphysis and epiphysis and during this period of growth, these outstrip ossification. When this ceases the growth of the bone stops. Injury can occur as a result of trauma which could be due to a "blow" incurred in a contact sport.

If we are to be successful in our efforts to avoid injuries to child sports participants, more emphasis needs to be exerted in the direction of preventative measures. Such measures can be taken by those who have the direct responsibility of working with children in sports activities. And this is the subject of the ensuing section of the chapter.

SUPERVISION

In the present context, the term *supervision* is essentially concerned with those persons who *coach* or *manage* children's sports teams. We are frequently asked by parents about the advisability of their children's participation in sports. The immediate response is to "check out" the qualifications and objectives of those persons who will assume the responsibility for coaching.

At one time this was a much more serious matter because many coaches have little experience – especially in how to deal with growing children in competitive situations.

At the present time, however, this situation has been alleviated somewhat, mainly because of such organizations as the *National Youth Sports Coaches Association* (NYSCA). This organization is a nonprofit association that has proven to be a frontrunner in the development of a national training system for volunteer sports youth coaches.

One of the authors' former students, Fred Engh, is the Association's President/CEO and he has provided us with materials, some of which we would like to pass on to the reader.

Around one half million coaches have undertaken the NYSCA's three-year, three-level program to qualify for membership and certification. This certification program focuses on helping volunteer coaches understand the physiological, physical, and emotional impact they have on children age 6 to 12. The criteria for NYSCA certification and membership are reviewed by the NYSCA National Executive Board which is comprised of representatives from the fields of education, recreation and sports law.

One of the important aspects of the NYSCA is the following "Coaches' Code of Ethics."

- I hereby pledge to live up to my certification as a NYSCA Coach by following the NYSCA Code of Ethics.
- I will place the emotional and physical well-being of my players ahead of any personal desire to win.
- I will remember to treat each player as an individual, remembering the large spread of emotional and physical development for the same age group.

- I will do my very best to provide a safe play situation for my players.
- I promise to review and practice the necessary first aid principles needed to treat injuries of my players.
- I will do my best to organize practices that are fun and challenging for all my players.
- I will lead, by example, in demonstrating fair play and sportsmanship to all my players.
- I will insure that I am knowledgeable in the rules of each sport that I coach, and that I will teach these rules to my players.
- I will use those coaching techniques appropriate for each of the skills that I teach.

One would hope that those coaches who supervise children's sports would have as their goal the best interest of the child.

In this regard, our own extensive surveys of children's sports participants on this subject have yielded some interesting results.

On a scale with 4.0 being the highest, boys rated their coaches at 3.4 and girls gave their coaches a 3.3 rating.

In answer to the question, "What do you like *best* about your coach?," boys gave the following most prominent answers.

The coach:

- is nice (34%)
- is fair (26%)
- teaches us good things (26%)
- is funny (7%)
- says it is all right if we lose (7%)

Girls gave the following answers to this question.
The coach:

- is nice (42%)
- is funny (28%)
- is fair (14%)
- helps us to play better (10%)
- is young (6%)

In answer to the question "What do you like *least* about your coach?," boys answered as follows.

The coach:

- gets mad and yells at us (64%)
- works us too hard (22%)
- doesn't let me play enough (8%)
- is not a good teacher (3%)
- doesn't praise us enough (3%)

Girls answered this question as follows.

The coach:

- gets mad and yells at us (57%)
- doesn't teach us much (19%)
- works us too hard (14%)
- doesn't praise us enough (5%)
- seems unhappy (5%)

In attempting to verbalize all of these data, one could come up with several possibilities of how children characterize their coach. Here is one such possibility. *The coach is usually a nice person with a sense of humor who is generally fair, but at the same time one who is likely to get mad and yell at the players.*

There is no question about it, the quality level of supervision is an important factor in children's sports. However, in the final analysis the success or failure of any program will ultimately depend upon its contribution to the total development of the child.

THE NEGATIVE ASPECT OF CHILDREN'S SPORTS

The negative dimension of children's sports is seen in such recent headlines as:

Coach Breaks Child's Arms
Child's Play – and Adult Rage

The previously mentioned Fred Engh once reported that he had witnessed much "ugliness in children's sports." He attributed this to vicarious parents who will stop at nothing to push their child unmercifully to be a star athlete and will cheat, bend the rules and even risk the safety of children. He maintained that this condition exists because many leagues are operated by parents who (1) have no official standards to allow equal play opportunity for children; (2) have no requirements that make it mandatory that coaches are trained and monitored for their behavior; (3) have no guidelines to prevent injuries and first aid procedures should injuries occur; and (4) have no policy that states that adult volunteers are drug, alcohol and tobacco free at youth sports activities. To this end Engh's *National Youth Sports Coaches Association* has developed the following "Parents' Code of Ethics."

- I hereby pledge to provide positive support, care and encouragement for my child participating in youth sports by following this Code of Ethics.
- I will encourage good sportsmanship by demonstrating positive support for all players, coaches, and officials at every age, practice or other youth sports event.
- I will place the emotional and physical well-being of my child ahead of any personal desire to win.
- I will insist that my child plays in a safe and healthy environment.
- I will provide support for coaches and officials working with my child to provide a positive, enjoyable experience for all.
- I will demand a drug-, alcohol- and tobacco-free sports environment for my child and agree to assist by refraining from their use at all youth sports events.
- I will remember that the game is for the children and not for adults.

- I will do my very best to make youth sports fun for my child.
- I will ask my child to treat other players, coaches, fans, and officials with respect regardless of race, sex, creed, or ability.
- I will promise to help my child enjoy the youth sports experience within my personal constraints by assisting with coaching, being a respectful fan, providing transportation or whatever I am capable of doing.
- I will require that my child's coach be trained in the responsibilities of being a youth sports coach and that the coach agree to the youth sports Coaches' Code of Ethics.
- I will read the NYSCA National Standards for Youth Sports and do everything in my power to assist all youth sports organizations and enforce them.

Parent Signature	Parent Signature	Date

In closing this chapter, we are pleased to report on an excellent study by researchers Douglan Horschhorn and Teri Loughead[8] that is very pertinent to this discussion. They examined the two main approaches that parents take in dealing with their child's participation in sports – "supportive and non-interfering" and "overbearing and stress causing."

Supportive and Non-Interfering Parents tended to follow these principles.

- Define winning by the level of effort, not the score of the game.
- Maintain open communication with the child throughout the sport experience.
- Establish ground rules for the child, with appropriate consequences for breaking them.
- Model appropriate behavior for the child.
- Allow the child to experience the dynamics of the sport at his or her own pace.
- Provide unconditional love and support regardless of the child's success or failure in the sport.

Overbearing and Stress Causing Parents tended to follow these principles:

- Try to live out their own athletic dreams through the child.
- Believe their child's success and failure in a sport is a reflection of their parenting ability.
- Send the message to the child that their love, support, and approval is dependent on the child's level of performance on the playing field.
- Are quick to criticize and slow to praise.
- May use age-inappropriate motivational techniques or drills with the child that can lead to overuse injuries or lowered self-esteem.
- Are cold and critical, which leads to a detrimental youth sport experience.

Finally, if those adults who are involved in children's sports expect to be successful they might well be guided by the positive aspects set forth in this chapter.

ENDNOTES

1. Horney, Karen, *The Neurotic Personality of Our Times*, New York, W. W. Norton & Company, Inc., 1937. (Cited to illustrate the considerable history of the concept.)
2. Kohn, A., *No Contest: The Case Against Competition*, Boston, Houghton-Miffin, 1986.
3. Scanlan, Tara K., and Passer, M. W., *The Psychological and Social Affect of Competition*, Los Angeles, University of California, 1977.
4. Scanlan, Tara K., Social Psychological Aspects of Competition for Male Youth Participants: Predictors of Competitive Stress, *Journal of Sport Psychology*, 6, 1984.
5. Youth Sports Deaths, *The AAALF Active Voice, Newsletter of the American Association for Active Lifestyles and Fitness*, 1, Fall 2000, p. 6.
6. Davis, Robert G., and Isaacs, Larry D., *Elementary Physical Education*, Winston-Salem, NC, Hunter Textbooks, Inc., 1992.
7. Orland, R. G., Soccer-Related Eye Injuries in Children and Adolescents, *Physician and Sportsmedicine*, November 1988.

8. Hirschhorn, Douglas Kamin, and Loughead, Teri Olisky, Parental Impact on Youth Participation in Sport, *Journal of Physical Education, Recreation and Dance*, November/December 2000, p. 26.

Chapter 2

PHILOSOPHY AND OBJECTIVES
OF CHILDREN'S SPORTS

Whether they are aware of it or not, all individuals have developed some kind of philosophy of life. They may not have put it into words, but their philosophy is exhibited in their daily actions.

Regardless of the professional or personal interest endeavor in which one chooses to engage, he or she will have some sort of philosophy about the endeavor. Hence, those persons who are involved in children's sports maintain a philosophy about this activity. The development of such a philosophy should begin before or soon after one begins to prepare to become involved in children's sports. One's philosophy need not necessarily remain static and may be subject to change as he or she gains experience and understanding or as the perceived expectations of society change in regard to the endeavor.

In line with developing a philosophy one needs to give very serious consideration to *the objectives of children's sports*. This is to say that it is necessary to have an understanding of the potential contributions children's sports can make to participants and to proceed in a manner whereby these contributions might be realized.

MEANING OF TERMS

A standard dictionary definition of the term *philosophy* usually refers to it as a pursuit of wisdom or enlightenment. Another generalized description of the term is that it concerns our fundamental beliefs or practicing those things in which we believe. More specifically, a philosophy of children's sports is concerned with a careful, systematic intellectual endeavor in which we attempt to see these sports as a whole and at the same time as an integral part of our culture.

The term *objective* appears to have been adopted by education from the military. The latter uses it to identify an area to be assaulted and/or captured in some way. The *Dictionary of Education* gives the following definition of the term: "Aim, end in view, or purpose of a course of action or a belief; that which is anticipated as desirable in the early phases of an activity and serves to select, regulate, and direct later aspects of the activity so that the total process is designed and integrated."[1]

It is noted that various other terms are used to convey the same meaning. Some of these include, *aim*, *goal*, and *purpose*. Regardless of the term used, we might well consider it with regard to a very simple meaning; that is, where are we trying to go or what are we trying to accomplish through the medium of children's sports?

DEVELOPING A PHILOSOPHY AND FORMULATING OBJECTIVES

Until about the twelfth century, few European sailors were willing to sail far beyond the sight of land because on the open sea they had no uniformly reliable way of knowing whether they were on course or not. Then the compass became known in Europe. From that time on seamen had something to sail by and thus could travel in all kinds of weather with considerable confidence that they were moving in the direction they wished. The compass made possible the exploration feats of such people as Columbus and Magellan, who first sailed around the world.

Those in the field of children's sports also need something to guide their efforts, a guiding philosophy so to speak. Otherwise they are like sailors of long ago who sometimes sailed about aimlessly and without confidence of their course when away from land. At times individuals involved in children's sports need to be able to "check the course" by referring to a compass in their own minds so as to know if they are moving in the proper direction. In order to do this they must have a "magnetic north" composed of a purpose and of clearly defined worthwhile objectives. If they have their worthy objectives in mind as they make decisions about their programs, they will not be sailing blind. If they do not, they will have no basis for knowing whether or not they are doing the right thing and making wise decisions.

This problem of philosophy and objectives applies to living in general. Many people are unhappy and feel their lives are empty simply because they have never thought out for themselves what is important to them and what they really wish to achieve in life. Without a philosophy to guide their thinking and actions they are like sea voyagers without a compass, off course they feel lost. Similarly, in those situations where sports experiences are not very effective, there is a very good chance that the people in charge are confused about the purpose of their work and are failing to operate in terms of desirable and worthwhile objectives.

Above all, objectives should always be in the best interest of the individual. This precludes the practice of some coaches using an injured player simply because their philosophy is concerned only with winning.

The approach taken here is that children's sports should be looked upon as a means of providing experiences which benefit the *whole* person; that is, sports have objectives which apply to the *total personality* of those who participate in them.

THE CONCEPT OF TOTAL PERSONALITY DEVELOPMENT

A great deal of clinical and experimental evidence indicates that a human being must be considered as a whole and not a collection of parts. Some terms used to describe this situation are "whole child," "unified individual," and "total personality." The latter term is commonly used in the fields of mental health and psychology and is gaining usage in the field of education.

Moreover, when we consider it from a point of view of one existing as a person, it is interesting to note that "existence as a person" is a rather common term used in definitions of personality.

What then comprises the total personality? Anyone who has difficulty in formulating views with regard to what the human personality actually consists of can take courage in the knowledge that many experts who spend their time studying this subject are not always in complete agreement as to what it is or how it operates. Indeed, one of the greatest mysteries which confronts man in modern society is man himself. If one were to analyze the literature on the subject it would be found generally that the total personality consists of the sum of all the *physical, social, emotional,* and *intellectual* aspects of an individual. The total personality is *one* thing comprising these various major aspects. All of these components are highly interrelated and interdependent. All are of importance to the balance and health of the personality because only in terms of their health can the personality as a whole maintain a completely healthy state. The condition of any one aspect affects each other aspect to a degree and hence the personality as a whole.

When a nervous person stutters or becomes nauseated, a mental state is *not* causing a physical symptom. On the contrary, a pressure imposed upon the organism causes a series of reactions which include thought, verbalization, digestive processes, and muscular function. Mind does not cause the body to become upset; the *total* organism is upset by a situation and reflects this condition of being upset in several ways, including disturbance in thought, feelings, and bodily processes. The whole individual responds in interaction with the social and physical environment. As the individual is affected by the environment, he or she in turn has an effect upon it.

However, because of a long tradition during which physical development *or* intellectual development, rather than physical *and* intellectual development has been celebrated, indeed glorified, we oftentimes are accustomed to dividing the two in our thinking. The result may be that we sometimes pull human being apart with this kind of thinking.

Traditional attitudes which separate mind and body tend to lead to unbalanced development of an individual with respect to mind and body and/or social adjustment. To understand better the concept of total personality the human organism can be seen in terms of the diagram in Figure 1.

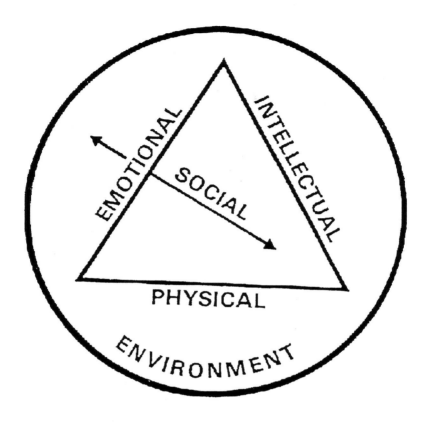

Figure 1. Schematic Diagram of the Total Personality

The circle is the total environment of the individual which circumscribes and confines all aspects of the total personality. The triangle with its three sides – physical, emotional, and intellectual aspects of the total personality – form a single figure with the *physical* aspect as the base. An arrow, extending from the center of the triangle upward through one of the sides, is designated *social* to represent interpersonal relationships within the field of the individual and the environment. The arrow is pointed at both ends to suggest a two-way process; the individual is affected by those around him or her and in turn has some affect upon them. The triangle is dependent upon a balance of all its parts, and if one part of the triangle is changed, the entire triangle is reshaped. It is interesting to draw diagrams in which one after the other of the sides is shortened – and see how this affects the triangle. It is also interesting to make personal application such as the following: What happens to my intellectual performance when I am worried or have a stomachache? What changes occur in my body when I feel frightened, embarrassed, or angered?

It is interesting that in modern times, when great emphasis is placed upon social adjustment, that perhaps a major problem involves faulty interpersonal relationships. For this reason it is important to make special note of the interaction between the individual and the environment. The quality of the individual's interpersonal relationships affects all the other aspects of his or her personality. How well do you drive a car when someone is shouting at you? How well can you concentrate when you think someone is talking about you? These are social circumstances which affect the physical, emotional and intellectual aspects of personality.

This matter of interpersonal relationships is still more fundamental to development of individuals than the foregoing illustration suggests. It has been found that infants and very young children who are deprived of a reasonable amount of mothering – that initial and basic social experience – actually stop growing in one or more aspects of their total personality, even though all of their needs are met. Some fail to develop mentally; some show both physical immaturity and mental retardation.

Still others are affected mainly at the emotional level. That is, if they are deprived of love and given instead non-loving care, they may fail to grow emotionally and not be capable of human feeling as we generally think of it. In brief, the quality of interpersonal relationships in the early years may tend to set the pattern of subsequent attitudes and behavior toward other people, authority, and the "rules of the game of life," generally.

All of these things then are the basis of total personality – a complex balance of psychophysical, and adventuresome living.

The foregoing statements have attempted to point out rather forcefully that the identified components of the total personality – physical, social, emotional, and intellectual – characterize the totality of being. The fact that each of these aspects might be considered as a separate entity needs to be taken into account. Because of this, each aspect warrants a separate discussion. This appears to be extremely important if one is to understand fully the place of each aspect as an integral part of the whole personality.

As these aspects of total personality are discussed, there will emerge objectives of children's sports as they relate to the various aspects. There will emerge a *physical objective* of children's sports, a *social objective* of children's sports, an *emotional objective* of children's sports, and an *intellectual objective* of children's sports. The reason for this approach to the formulating of objectives of children's sports lies in the fact that in order to make a valid exploration of the area of children's sports in the out-of-school setting, it becomes necessary to consider the guiding philosophy and purpose of education as a whole. The necessity of this consideration becomes most important when one takes into account that the basic philosophy which guides any program should also apply to children's sports.

If one were to analyze the various statements of purpose of the whole of education which have been made by responsible groups through the years, it would be a relatively easy matter to identify a constantly emerging pattern. These statements have gradually evolved into a more or less general agreement that the general goal of education is to stimulate and guide the growth of an individual so that he or she will function in life activities that involve vocation, citizenship, and enriched leisure; and further stimulate the individual so that he or she will possess as high a level of physical, social, emotional, and intellectual development as the individual capacity will permit. If it is a valid assumption that the purpose of education is to attempt to insure development of the total personality, then it is incumbent upon those in children's sports to explore these developmental processes as they relate to sports.

THE PHYSICAL ASPECT OF PERSONALITY

One obvious point of departure in discussing the physical aspect of personality could be to state that "everybody has a body." Some are short, some are tall, some are lean, and some are fat. Children come in different sizes, but all of them have a certain innate capacity which is influenced by the environment.

As far as any individual is concerned, it might be said that he or she *is* his or her body. It is the base of operation – what was previously referred to as the "physical base." The other components of the total personality – social, emotional, and intellectual – are somewhat vague as far as some individuals are concerned. Although these are manifested in various ways, a person does not necessarily see them as he or she does the physical aspect. Consequently, it becomes exceedingly important that one be helped early in life to gain control over the physical aspect, to develop what is known as basic body discipline and control. The willingness and ability to do this of course will vary greatly from one person to another. It will depend, for example, upon the status of physical fitness of the individual. The broad area of physical fitness can be broken down into certain components, and it is important that individual achieve fitness to the best of their natural ability as far as these components are concerned. There is not complete agreement as far as identification of the components of physical fitness is concerned. However, the following information provided by the President's Council on Physical Fitness and Sports considers certain components to be basic as follows.

1. *Muscular strength*. This refers to the contraction power of the muscles. The strength of muscles is usually measured with dynamometers or tensiometers which record the amount of force particular muscle groups can apply in a single maximum effort. Man's existence and relative physical effectiveness depend upon the muscles. All movements of the body or any of its parts are impossible without action by muscles attached to the skeleton. Muscles perform vital functions of the body as well. The heart is a muscle. Death occurs when it ceases to contract. Breathing, digestion, and elimination are impossible without muscular contractions. These vital muscular functions are influenced by exercising the skeletal muscles; the heart beats faster, the blood circulates through the body at a greater rate, breathing becomes deep and rapid, and perspiration breaks out on the surface of the skin.

2. *Muscular endurance*. Muscular endurance is the ability of muscles to exert themselves and to perform work. Two variations of muscular endurance are recognized: *Isometric* whereby a maximum static muscular contraction is held and *isotonic* whereby the muscles continue to raise and lower a submaximal load as in weight training or performing push-ups. In the isometric form, they alternately shorten and lengthen. Muscular endurance must assume some muscular strength. However, there are

distinctions between the two; muscle groups of the same strength may possess different degrees of endurance.

3. *Circulatory-respiratory endurance.* Circulatory-respiratory endurance is characterized by moderate contractions of large muscle groups for relatively long periods of time during which maximal adjustments of the circulatory-respiratory system to the activity are necessary, as in distance running and swimming. Obviously, strong and enduring muscles are needed. However, by themselves they are not enough; they do not guarantee well-developed circulatory-respiratory functions. This is frequently discussed in terms of cardiovascular function and cardiovascular fitness.

In addition to the basic three above, there are other components of physical fitness to be considered:

1. *Muscular power.* Ability to release maximum muscular force in the shortest time. Examples: Standing long jump and the sudden, explosive blocking function in football.

2. *Agility.* Speed in changing body positions or in changing direction. Example: The dodging run.

3. *Speed.* Rapidity with which successive movements of the same kind can be performed. Example: 50-yard dash.

4. *Flexibility.* Range of movements in a joint or a sequence of joints. Example: Touch fingers to floor without bending knees.

5. *Balance.* Ability to maintain position and equilibrium both in movement (dynamic balance) and while stationary (static balance). Examples: Walking on a line or balance beam (dynamic), standing on one foot (static).

6. *Coordination.* Working together of the muscles and organs of the human body in the performance of a specific task. Example: Throwing or catching an object.

The components of physical fitness and hence the physical aspect of personality can be measured with calibrated instruments, as in the case of measuring muscle strength mentioned above. Moreover, we can tell how tall or heavy one is at any stage of development. We can derive other accurate data with measurements of blood pressure, blood counts, urinalysis, and the like.

PHYSICAL OBJECTIVES

It may be generally stated that a good program of children's sports can be considered a stimulant to physical growth. Further, the general consensus indicates that participation in a well-balanced children's sports program is an important way of maintaining optimum health.

Two major objectives emerge as far as the physical aspect of personality is concerned. The first of these takes into account *maintaining a suitable level of physical fitness*. Second, there is a consideration of the *development of skill and ability*.

Maintaining a Suitable Level of Physical Fitness

Physical fitness presupposes among other things an adequate intake of nutritious food and an adequate amount of rest and sleep; but beyond these things activity involving all the big muscles of the body is essential. Just how high a level of physical fitness should be maintained from one stage to another is difficult to determine because we must raise the question: "Fitness for what?"

Physical fitness has been described in many different ways by different people. However, when all of these descriptions are carefully considered it is likely that they will be characterized more by their similarities than by their differences. For purposes here we will think of physical fitness as the level of ability of the human organism to perform certain physical tasks. Or, stated another way, the fitness to perform various specified tasks requiring muscular effort.

Development of Skill and Ability

The second major physical objective of children's sports has to do with disciplined body movement. The physically educated individual, commensurate with his or her capacity and within his or her own limitations, is adept in a variety of sports activities. We enjoy those activities in which we are reasonable proficient. We are dealing with an important principle here related to our sports objectives. That is, if people are to enjoy participating in an activity, they need to be reasonably competent in the skills involved in the activity. Consequently, there must be objectives both in terms of the *number* of skills to which children are introduced and the level of competence to be achieved so that they will associate a pleasurable experience with participation.

We must reckon with another matter that is closely related to competence in a wide variety of skills. Some physical education teachers have stressed the very strenuous team sports in their school programs and others have placed emphasis on what have been called "life-time sports" which may be used later on in life. A sensible point of view on this subject would appear to be that we should develop competence in a variety of skills for use *now and in the future.* Stated more specifically, as an objective of children's sports it could be said that all individuals should be prepared by their sports experience to participate in suitable and satisfying activities for use now and in the future.

In summary, the physical objective of children's sports should imply organic development commensurate with vigor, vitality, strength, balance, flexibility, and neuromuscular coordination, together with the development of skill and ability in a variety of activities for use both now and in the future.

THE SOCIAL ASPECT OF PERSONALITY

Human beings are social beings. They work together for the benefit of society. They have fought together in times of national emergencies in order to preserve the kind of society they believe in, and they play together. While all this may be true, the social aspect of personality still is not clearly delineated or defined and is sometimes confusing as far as young children are concerned.

It was a relatively easy matter to identify certain components of physical fitness such as strength and endurance. However, this does not necessarily hold true for components of social fitness. The components for physical fitness are the same for children as adults. On the other hand, the components of social fitness for children may be different from the components of social fitness for adults. By some adult standards, children might be considered social misfits because some of their behavior might not be socially acceptable to some adults.

To the chagrin of some adults, parents as well as teachers, children are likely to be uninhibited as far as the social aspect of personality is concerned. In this regard we need to be concerned with social maturity as it pertains to the growing and ever changing individual. This is to say that we need to give consideration to certain characteristics of social maturity and how well they are dealt with at the different stages of growth and development of children.

Perhaps we need to ask ourselves such questions as these: Are we helping children to become self-reliant by giving them independence at the proper time? Are we helping them to be outgoing and interested in others as well as themselves? Are we helping them to know how to satisfy their own needs in a socially desirable way? Are we helping them to develop a wholesome attitude toward themselves and others?

Social maturity and hence social fitness might well be expressed in terms of fulfillment of certain social needs. In other words, if certain social needs are being adequately met, children should be in a better position to realize social fitness. Among the needs we must give consideration to are (1) the *need for affection* which involves acceptance and approval by persons, (2) the *need for belonging* which involves acceptance and approval of the group, and (3) the *need for mutuality* which involves cooperation, mutual helpfulness and group loyalty.

When it comes to evaluating the social aspect of personality we do not have the same kind of objective and calibrated instruments that are available in assessing the physical aspect of personality. Mainly for diagnostic purposes in their dealings with children some teachers have successfully used some of the sociometric techniques. At best, however, the social aspect of personality is difficult to appraise objectively because of its somewhat nebulous nature.

SOCIAL OBJECTIVES

The sports "laboratory" (areas where activities take place) should present near ideal surroundings and environment for social development of children. Why are people in the field of children's sports convinced that this area provides some of the very best means for teaching vital social skills? By their very nature sports activities are essentially socially oriented. The team sports are obviously so, but so too are activities such as gymnastics, swimming, tennis and golf. It is important to note that when children engage in sports, they will be participating actually in social experiences. If any type of play is to be successful and satisfying, the people involved must possess or acquire considerable skill in dealing with one another. They must learn to work together in the interest of the team. They must learn to accept and respect the rules of the games that they play. They must learn that sometimes it is necessary to place the welfare of the team ahead of their own personal desires. They must respect the rights of others. They must be loyal to their group. They must think and plan with the group and for the group. They must learn to win and lose gracefully.

In looking back over this list of social skills that are "musts" in children's sports, it should be discerned that it is just such social skills which are necessary for happy and successful social living everywhere. A certain level of social skills on the part of each performer is absolutely essential if play is to be successful. Everyone knows, for example, what the effects of a "poor sport" are upon friendly games. A qualified coach finds numerous opportunities to develop skills of interpersonal relationships which far exceed the basic essentials for successful play. Indeed, men and women coaches should consider the development of increased social awareness and social skills as important objectives of their programs, and they should make specific plans to reach these objectives. They should recognize that sports activities can have a profoundly humanizing effect upon children, in that participants learn to evaluate their teammates and opponents on the basis of what they can do and what kinds of persons they are rather than on the basis of their looks, their race, their religion, their color, or their economic status.

The Emotional Aspect of Personality

In introducing the subject of emotion we are confronted with the fact that for many years it has been a difficult concept to define. In addition there have been many changing ideas and theories as far as the study of emotion is concerned.

Obviously, it is not the purpose of a book of this nature to attempt to go into great depth on a subject that has been one of the most intricate undertakings of psychology for many years. A few general statements relative to the nature of emotion do appear to be in order if we are to understand more clearly this aspect of personality as it concerns children's sports.

Emotion may be described as a response a person makes to a stimulus for which he or she is not prepared or which suggests a possible source of gain or loss. For example, if an individual is confronted with a situation and does not have a satisfactory response, the emotional pattern of fear may result; if a person is in a position where desires are frustrated, the emotional pattern of anger may occur.

This line of thought suggests that emotions might be classified in two different ways – those which are *pleasant* and those which are *unpleasant*. For example, *joy* could be considered a pleasant emotional experience while *fear* would be an unpleasant one. It is interesting to note that a good proportion of the literature is devoted to emotions that are unpleasant. It has been found that in psychology textbooks much more space is given to such emotional patterns as fear, hate, guilt, and anxiety than to such pleasant emotions as love, sympathy, and contentment.

Generally speaking, the pleasantness or unpleasantness of an emotion seems to be determined by its strength or intensity, by the nature of the situation arousing it, and by the way an individual perceives or interprets the situation. As far as young children are concerned, their emotions tend to be more intense and sometimes more overwhelming, than those of adults. If an adult is not aware of this aspect of child behavior, he or she will not likely understand why a child may react inattentively or even violently to a situation that to an adult seems somewhat insignificant. The fact that different individuals will react differently to the same type of situation also should be taken into account; for example, something that might anger one person might have a rather passive influence on another individual. In this regard, it is interesting to observe the effect that winning or losing a game has on certain children.

When we attempt to evaluate the emotional aspect of personality, we tend to encounter much the same situation as when we attempt to evaluate the social aspect. But perhaps the emotional aspect is even more difficult to evaluate than the social aspect. Included among some of the methods used for attempting to measure emotional responses are the following:

1. *Blood pressure.* It rises when one is under some sort of emotional stress.
2. *Blood sugar analysis.* Under stressful conditions more sugar enters the blood stream.
3. *Pulse rate.* Emotional stress causes it to elevate.
4. *Galvanic skin response.* Similar to the lie detector technique and measurements are recorded in terms of perspiration on palms of hands.

These as well as others have been used by investigators of human emotion and they have various and perhaps limited degrees of validity. In attempting to assess emotional reactivity we often encounter the problem of the extent to which we are dealing with a purely physiological response or a purely emotional response. For example, one's pulse rate could be elevated by taking some sort of physical exercise. It could likewise be elevated if a person were the object of an embarrassing remark by another. Thus in this illustration the elevation of pulse could be caused for different reasons, the first being physiological and the second being emotional. Then too, the type of emotional pattern is not identified by the measuring device. A joy response and an anger response could show the same or nearly the same rise in pulse rate. These are some of the reasons why it is most difficult to arrive at a high degree of objectivity in studying the emotional aspect of personality.

EMOTIONAL OBJECTIVES

Most everyone recognizes that sports contests are highly emotionalized situations for both participants and spectators. For the participant, there is the excitement before a contest. When play is in progress there is the exhilaration of making skillful moves and plays, and the disappointments at being frustrated or bested by an opponent. Finally, the after-play emotions are determined to some extent by how well the participant performed in relation to how well he or she thinks they can perform, but in almost all instances the pleasurable emotions are caused at least in part by the positive feeling that the time has been well spent. As for the spectator, he or she is likely to be swept by powerful feelings of excitement, joy, anger, and disappointments from the start to the finish of an intense contest. Many sociologists are tending to believe that spectators find in their favorite sport some of the thrills, excitement, and triumphs that are missing from the rest of their lives, and thus sports are of great importance to them.

With regard to sports objectives there is a least one highly important outcome that might well be accomplished as far as the emotional aspect of personality is concerned. That is, to develop in children an increased capacity to control their emotions, *both as participants and as spectators*, and thus contributing to the development of their emotional balance and maturity. (A similar point might also be made with regard to some adult coaches of children's sports.)

Emotional Control

It could be said that a major difference between you and some criminals confined to prison is that you have the ability to control your emotional impulses to a greater extent than they. Perhaps all of us at one time or another have experienced the same kinds of emotions that have led the abnormal individual into committing violence, but we have been able to hold our powerful and violent emotions in check. This may be an extreme example, but it should suggest something of the importance of emotional control in modern society.

It would appear that a reasonable and natural objective of sports should be to help participants increase their capacity to handle and control their emotions. The thoughtful coach is aware of educational opportunities offered in sports situations for children, both as participants and spectators, to learn to deal with their own emotional arousals *in socially acceptable ways*. He or she can try to guide children in such a way that they learn to take pride in their ability to restrain themselves when necessary in order to abide by the rules of fair play and to behave like reasonable and decent human beings. The coach has real emotionally charged situations with which to work in order to teach children to deal with strong emotions. Unfortunately, it cannot be said unequivocally that all coaches are taking very great advantage of an excellent opportunity. In fact, studies show that spectator problems in children's sports often are influenced by the behavior of the coach during games and thus is sometimes a primary determinate in how spectators behave.

Another aspect of controlling the emotions is becoming able to function effectively and intelligently in an emotionally charged situation. Sport success hinges upon this ability as does success in many other life situations. Extremes of emotional upset must be avoided if the individual is to be able to think and act effectively. In sports situations children should learn that if they immediately put their minds to work on other things, such as team strategy, they can then control their emotions.

It is sometimes helpful to visualize your emotions as being forces within you which are in a struggle for power with your mind as to which is to control you – your reason or your emotions. Oftentimes our basic emotions are blind and unconcerned with the welfare of other people or sometimes even with our own welfare. Emotional maturity has to do with gaining increased mastery over our emotions – not, or course, eliminating them – so that we may behave as intelligent and balanced human beings rather than as out of control individuals.

In summarizing emotional objectives of sports, it could be said that these objectives should imply that sympathetic and effective guidance should be provided in meeting anxieties, joys, and sorrows and also that help given in developing aspirations, affections and security.

THE INTELLECTUAL ASPECT OF PERSONALITY

The word intelligence is derived from the Latin word *intellectus* which literally means the "power of knowing." The term *intelligence* has been described in many ways. One general description of it is the capacity to learn or understand.

Individuals posses varying degrees of intelligence, with most people falling within a range of what is called "normal" intelligence. In dealing with this aspect of personality we should perhaps give attention to some components of *intellectual fitness*. However, this is difficult to do. Because of the somewhat amorphic nature of intelligence, it is practically impossible to identify specific components of it. Therefore, we need to view intellectual fitness in a somewhat different manner.

For purposes of this discussion, we will consider intellectual fitness from two different, but closely related points of view. First, from a standpoint of intellectual *needs* and second, from a standpoint of how certain things *influence* intelligence. It might be said that if a person's intellectual needs are being met, then he or she is intellectually fit. From the second point of view, if we know how certain things influence intelligence then we might understand better how to contribute to intellectual fitness by improving upon these factors.

There appears to be some rather general agreement with regard to the intellectual needs of human beings. Among others, these needs include (1) a need for challenging experiences at the individual's level of ability, (2) a need for intellectually successful and satisfying experiences, (3) a need for the opportunity to solve problems, and (4) a need for the opportunity to participate in creative experiences rather than always having to conform to generally accepted norms.

Some of those factors which tend to influence intelligence are (1) health and physical condition, (2) emotional disturbance, and (3) certain social and .

When coaches have an understanding of intellectual needs and factors influencing intelligence, perhaps then they can deal satisfactorily with children in assisting them with the intellectual dimension of their pursuits in sports.

INTELLECTUAL OBJECTIVES

Of the contributions that sports might make to the development of total personality, the one concerned with intellectual development has been the one most subjected to criticism by some educators. Close scrutiny of the possibilities of intellectual development through sports reveals, however, that a very desirable contribution can be made through the experience of sports.

In a well-coached sports activity there are numerous opportunities to exercise judgment and resort to reflective thinking in the solution of various kinds of problems. In addition, individuals must acquire a knowledge of rules and regulations that govern sports contests. It is also essential for effective participation that individuals gain an understanding of the various fundamentals and strategy involved in the performance of sports activities. Perhaps more importantly is the fact that all of the systems of perception are inherent in most sports experiences. This means that these experiences provide for improvement upon such perceptual-motor qualities as auditory and visual perception skills and kinesthetic and tactile perception skills. All of these factors say to us that there is present an integral intellectual component in sports.

In summary, there is no question that the development of a sound philosophy and the formulation of valid objectives in each of these areas – physical, social, emotional and intellectual – is perhaps the most important aspect of a successful children's sports program. It is believed that the suggestions set forth in this chapter will be of use to those individuals who have major responsibilities in the worthy enterprise of children's sports.

ENDNOTE

1. Good, Carter V., *Dictionary of Education*, New York, McGraw-Hill, 1959, p. 371.

Chapter 3

BASIC SPORTS SKILLS PATTERNS

In many cases people make the mistake of labeling a certain condition as luck – good or bad – when in reality the condition is a breakdown in skill performance. Several years ago the first author conducted an observational study of what was termed as *sports errors*. In well over 90 percent of the cases these errors were the fault of poor skill performance. A player fumbles a football because he did not have the skill or proper technique to hold on to the ball. A fielder misses a fly ball because of inability to catch it, and on and on. Thus adults should not subscribe to the theory of bad luck when the cause is a lack of or deficiency in skill. A major function of this chapter is to consider the biomechanics of certain basic movement skills and their importance to successful sports participation for children.

Just as the perception of symbols is concerned with reading readiness, so is basic movement an important factor in readiness to perform in various kinds of sports activities. Since proficient performance in sports activities is dependent upon skill of body movement, the ability of the child to move effectively should be readily discerned.

Skills are the scientific way to move the body and/or its segments in such a way as to expend a minimum amount of energy requirement, but achieve maximum results. Performance of specific skills has been arrived at by scientific insight from such fields as anatomy and kinesiology, which suggests to us how the body can move to achieve maximum efficiency.

Other things being equal, the degree of proficient performance of a skill by an individual is directly related to his or her innate capacity; that is, each individual is endowed with a certain amount of native ability. Through such factors as good teaching, motivation and guided practice, attempts are made to help the child perform to the best of his or her individual ability and maintain the highest *skill level* at which the child is reasonably capable of performing.

FACTORS INVOLVED IN SKILL TEACHING AND LEARNING

Although each child is born with a certain potential capacity, we should not subscribe to the notion that skills are a part of the child's inheritance. Skills must be learned. In order that a child can participate satisfactorily with peers, he or she must be given the opportunity to learn the skills under the careful guidance of competent adults.

Perhaps the ideal time to learn certain basic skills is in childhood. The muscular pliability of the young child is such that this is a desirable setting for the acquisition of various kinds of skills. The child is at a stage in life where there is usually adequate time for practice – a most important factor because children need practice in order to learn – and at this age level they do not seem to become weary of repeating the same practice routines over and over again. In addition, the young child has a limited number of established skills to obstruct the learning of new skills. Skill learning, therefore, should be facilitated provided competent teaching in the area of sports skills is available.

Experimental research on the influence of specific instruction on various kinds of skills is somewhat limited. More and more scientific evidence is being accumulated, however, which appears to indicate that children in the early elementary school years are mature enough to benefit from instruction in skills such as throwing, running and jumping.

Following are some suggested guidelines that adults might take into account in the instruction of skills.

1. The adult should become familiar with the skills involved in a given sports activity. This means that is will be necessary to analyze the activity to determine the type and the extent of the skill requirements.

2. In considering the development of sports skills, the adult should recognize that skills include the following three components: (a) preparing for the movement, (b) executing the movement, and (c) following through. For example, in throwing a ball the individual prepares for the movement by assuming the proper position to throw. Then he or she completes the actual throwing of the ball. Finally there is a follow-through action of the arm and torso after the ball leaves the hand. All of these elements are essential for satisfactory performance of this particular skill.

3. The skill should be taught correctly from the beginning. Otherwise children may have to do a considerable amount of 'unlearning' at a later stage of development.

4. When an error in skill performance is observed, it should be corrected immediately. This can be done under the guidance of the adult by evaluating the child's performance. Correction of errors in skill performance is essential, first because continued repetition may formulate the faulty practice into a fixed habit, and second because the child will have less difficulty learning more complex skills if he or she has previously learned easier skills correctly. Adults should recognize that while there are general patterns for the best performance of skills, individual differences may be considered. This implies that a child should be permitted to deviate from a standard if he or she is able to perform a skill satisfactorily in a manner peculiar to his or her own individual abilities.

5. The greatest amount of time should be spent on skill learning that involves immediate application. In other words, the child should have immediate use for sports skills being taught so that he or she can properly apply them commensurate with the stage of development.

6. There is some indication that rhythmic accompaniment is important in the learning of skills. Although the evidence is not definitive and clear-cut, various studies tend to support this contention.

7. Two ways in which sports skills can be classified are *general* and *specific*. General sports skills are those which are used in many different team sports, while specific sports skills are those which are peculiar to a particular sport. For example, some form of *running* is used in most team

sports, while the skill of *spiking* is used specifically in the game of volleyball.

LOCOMOTOR SKILLS

Locomotor skills involve changes in body position that propel the body over the surface with the impetus being given by the feet and legs. Discussed here are four basic types of these skills: Running, leaping, jumping, hopping, plus two combination skills, which are galloping and sliding. The first four of these are performed with an even rhythm, and the last two are done with an uneven rhythm. Locomotor skills require a certain amount of strength and the development of the important sensory-motor mechanisms that are concerned with balance. They may also require various degrees of neuromotor coordination for proficient performance.

All of the locomotor skills should be learned correctly by children in the 6-12 age range. One reason is that these skills comprise the basic requirements for proficiency of performance in the activities contained in any well-planned team sports activity for children. Also, it is important that the child be helped early in life to gain control over the physical aspect of personality, or what is known as *basic body control*.

Adults should have certain basic knowledge about the locomotor skills so that they will be alert to improve performance of these skills. The following generalized information is intended for this purpose.

Running

At about 18 months of age, the average child develops a movement that appears to be in between a walk and a run. This is to say that the walking pattern is accelerated, but does not approximate running form. Usually, it is not before ages five or six that the child's running form becomes similar to that of an adult. As the child gets older he or she is able to increase the speed of running as well as be able to run greater distances.

Like walking, running involves transferring the weight from one foot to the other, but the rate of speed is increased. The ball of the foot touches the surface area first, and the toes point straight ahead. The body is momentarily suspended in the air when there is no contact with the surface area. This differs form the walk in which contact with either foot is always maintained with the surface area. In the run, there is more flexion at the knee, which involves a higher knee lift. There is also a higher arm lift, with flexion at the elbow reaching a point of about a right angle. In running, there is more of a forward lean than in walking, and in both cases the head points straight ahead. In many instances, the child who has not been taught to run correctly will violate certain mechanical principles by having a backward rather than forward lean, by carrying the arms to high, and by turning the head to the side rather than looking straight ahead.

Running is probably the most used of all the locomotor skills in the team game activities.

Some Ways Children Can Practice Running

1. Run in place.
2. Run straight ahead for a short distance as fast as you can.
3. Line up some lawn chairs or other objects and run around and between them.
4. Run to a point and stop; turn and run back.
5. With some friends, practice running while trying to keep out of each other's way.
6. Run for a distance; first fast and then slow.
7. Run alone throwing a ball into the air and catching it.
8. Run along with a partner.

Leaping

Leaping, like walking and running, is performed with an even rhythm like a slow run, with one essential difference; the push-off is up and then forward, with the feeling of suspension "up and over." The landing should be on the ball of the foot with sufficient flexion at the knee to absorb the shock. (Incidentally, most sports announcers use the term *leaping* incorrectly. They tend to conceive it as a movement for height, rather than what it really is – a forward locomotor movement. Thus they refer to come basketball players as "leapers" when they should be using the term "jumpers.")

Although leaping is not used frequently as a specific locomotor skill in many sports activities, there are certain reasons why it is important that children become proficient in this skill. For example, the leap can be combined with the run to leap over an object so as not to deviate from the running pattern. Sometimes this happens with football players leaping over another player on the ground. In addition, in retrieving a ball that has been thrown or hit high, a leap for the ball can help the child catch it "on the run" and thus continue the running pattern, rather than having to stop his or her movement.

Some Ways Children Can Practice Leaping

1. Run along, then leap with one foot and then the other foot.
2. Put something in front of you and then run and leap over it.
3. Put up several small boxes and run and leap over them first with one foot and then the other.
4. Do five or six leaps without any running steps in between.

Jumping

In a sense, jumping is somewhat like running in that the movement pattern is similar. However, jumping requires elevation of the body off the surface area, and thus more strength is needed to apply force for this purpose. Usually, the child's first experience with a movement approximating jumping occurs when he or she steps from a higher to a lower level, as in the case of going down stairs. Although there are many variations in jumping performance of children, generally speaking, they tend to improve their performance as they get older, with improvement tending to be more pronounced for boys than girls.

Jumping is accomplished by pushing off with both feet and landing on both feet or pushing off with one foot and landing on both feet. Since absorption of shock is important in jumping the landing should be with flexed knees and on the balls of the feet. Games such as basketball and volleyball require skill in jumping in order to increase proficiency in such activities.

Some Ways Children Can Practice Jumping

1. Stand in place and jump; go just a little bit higher each time.
2. Jump and take a little bit of a turn before you land.
3. Jump forward, sideward, and backward.
4. Make some circles or squares on the ground; jump from one to the other.
5. Get close to a wall and jump. Stretch your arm up high and remember where your fingers are. Now jump and touch the wall. Measure the distance between the fingers when standing and after the jump.
6. Put some small boxes up and jump over them.
7. Hold hands facing a partner; jump up and down while doing so.
8. Have two friends swing a rope while you jump over it.
9. Run a short distance to a line and jump; be sure you have a soft landing place.

Hopping

While hopping is the least difficult of the even, rhythmic locomotor skills to describe, at the same time it is perhaps the most difficult to execute. Hopping involves taking off and landing on the same foot. Thus, hopping is a more complex aspect of the jump because the body is elevated from the surface area by the action of only one foot. Not only is greater strength needed for the hop, but also more refined adjustment of balance is required because of the smaller base of support.

Even though hopping is not a specific skill used in most sports activities, one of the more important reasons why children should become proficient in this locomotor skill is that it can help them regain balance in any kind of activity where they have temporarily "lost their footing." When this occurs, the child can use the hop to keep his or her balance and remain in an upright position while getting the temporarily incapacitated foot into action. Adults can have children practice this as a drill.

Some Ways Children Can Practice Hopping

1. See how long you can stand on one foot.
2. See how long you can stand on the other foot.
3. Hop in place, first on one foot and then the other.
4. Hop and take a short turn.
5. Hop forward.
6. Hop sideward.
7. Hop backward.
8. Hop a short distance on one foot and back on the other.
9. Hop over a small box.

Galloping

The skill of galloping is a combination of the basic pattern of walking and leaping and is performed with an uneven rhythm. Since an uneven rhythmic movement requires more neuromotor coordination, the ability to gallop is developed later than those locomotor movements requiring an even rhythm. The child is likely to learn to gallop before he or she learns to skip, with about one-half of the children being able to perform at least an approximation of a galloping movement by about the age of four. Between the ages of six and seven most children can perform this movement.

Galloping can be explained by pretending that one foot is injured. A step is taken with the lead foot, but the "injured" foot can bear very little weight and is brought up only behind the other foot, and thus a fast limp is really a gallop.

Galloping is a skill that does not have prevalent use as a specific skill in most sports activities. One of the most important factors about learning to gallop is that it helps children to be able to change direction in a forward and backward plane more easily. Backward galloping can be done by starting with the lead foot to the back. If a child is proficient in galloping, he or she will likely be more successful in games that require a forward and/or backward movement for successful performance in that particular activity.

Some Ways Children Can Practice Galloping

1. Gallop forward for a short distance and stop quickly.
2. Gallop backward. You have to do this more slowly because you cannot see where you are going. Remember that you start backward with the lead foot.
3. Take about three gallops and then change your lead foot. You do this by taking a step with the trailing foot and making it the lead foot.
4. Gallop and see how close you can stay to the ground.
5. Gallop and see how high you can get. You will find that it is better to stay close to the ground.

Sliding

Sliding is much the same as the gallop but movement is in a sideward direction. One foot is drawn up to the lead foot; weight is shifted from the lead foot to the drawing foot and back again. As in the case of galloping, sliding is not used frequently as a specific skill in most sports activities. The important reason for gaining proficiency in the skill of sliding is that it helps the child to be able to change direction skillfully in a lateral plane. Many games involving guarding an opponent, such as basketball, require skill in sliding for success in the game. When a child has developed the skill of sliding from side to side, he or she does not have to cross the feet and thus can change direction laterally much more easily.

Some Ways Children Can Practice Sliding

1. Slide in one direction very slowly.
2. Slide in the other direction as quickly as you can.

3. Slide and see how quickly you can stop and slide the other way.
4. Slide and keep low to the ground.
5. Slide and raise yourself high off the ground – see how much better it is to keep close to the ground.
6. Get a partner and take his or her hand; try to slide together.
7. Slide with your partner without holding hands; see if you can stay close together as you face each other.
8. Get several friends and make a circle; join hands and slide one way in the circle and then the other way.

AXIAL SKILLS

Axial skills are non-locomotor in nature. They can be performed with some parts of the body remaining in contact with the surface area or the body as a whole in total movement. Included among the axial skills are swinging, bending, stretching, pulling, pushing, and the rotation movements of turning and twisting.

Each of these movements is required at one time or another in the performance of practically all sports activities. Proficiency of performance of the axial skills will improve performance in locomotor skills. For example, we are aware of the importance of arm swinging in running. When children can perform the axial skills with grace and facility there is a minimum expenditure of energy, with better performance results.

AUXILIARY SKILLS

There are certain skills that are not ordinarily classified as either locomotor or axial. However, they are highly important in the successful performance of many sports activities. These skills are arbitrarily identified here as auxiliary skills. Among some of the more important of this type of skill are starting, stopping, dodging, pivoting, falling and landing.

Starting

In activities that require responding to a stimulus, a quick start is an important element for success. How well a child will be able to "start" depends upon his or her reaction time and speed of movement. Reaction time is the amount of time that it takes from the time a signal is given until the onset of the initial movement. Speed of movement is concerned with how fast the person completes the initial movement. Although the factors concerned with starting are innate, they improve with practice. When an adult observes children as being "slow starters," additional help should be given to improve this skill.

Some Ways Children Can Practice Starting

1. Have a friend be a partner. Stand facing each other a short distance apart; have your feet close together. At a signal from your partner, move your foot out to the side about 12 inches. See how fast you react. See how fast you move your foot. Change, and you give the signal to your partner. Try giving a signal by sound, such as calling, "Go!" Also give a signal by sight by waving an arm as the signal to start. See if it takes longer to start with the sound signal or the sight signal.
2. Start to run as fast as you can. Then start to run in slow motion. You can see the difference between a fast start and a slow start.

Stopping

The skill of stopping is very important because all locomotor movements culminate with this skill. Numerous sports activities require a quick stop for successful performance.

Two ways of stopping are the *stride* stop and the *skip* stop. The stride stop involves stopping in running stride. There is flexion at the knees and a slight backward lean to maintain balance. This method of stopping can be used when the performer is moving at a slow speed. The skip stop should be used when there is fast movement, and the performer needs to come to a quick stop. This is accomplished with a hop on either foot, with the other foot making contact with the surface area almost simultaneously. Because of the latter movement, this method of stopping is sometimes called the *jump stop*, because ti appears that the performer is landing on both feet at the same time.

Some Ways Children Can Practice Stopping

1. Run along and stop.
2. Run along and have someone give you a signal to stop. Have them give you a signal to start and then stop again.
3. Run to a wall and stop just before you get there. See if you did a good job of judging when to stop.
4. Run around in a circle and keep changing directions. Have someone give you a signal of when to stop and when to start again.
5. Get together with some friends and play the game "Start and Stop." In this game several players stand in a line side by side. One person is chosen to be the leader and stands at a goal line some distance away; the leader calls, "Start!" On this signal the players run forward. The leader calls, "Stop!" Anyone moving after this signal must return to the starting line. This game can go on until one player has reached the goal line. Play the game the same way but use a sight signal rather than a sound signal. The leader can signal by waving the arm or a piece of cloth.

Dodging

Dodging involves changing direction while running. The knees are bent, and the weight is transferred in the dodging direction; this movement is sometimes called "veering" or "weaving." After a dodge is made, the performer can continue in the different direction with a push-off from the surface area with the foot to which the weight was previously transferred. The importance of skill in dodging is seen in games where getting away from an opponent is necessary.

Some Ways Children Can Practice Dodging

1. Run to a certain point and change direction by dodging.
2. Set up several objects and dodge around them.
3. With a partner, run up to him or her and dodge around the partner.
4. Play a game of tag with some friends and see how important it is to be able to dodge.
5. Have someone toss a ball at you and try to dodge it.

Pivoting

Whereas dodging is used to change direction during body movement, pivoting is employed to change direction while the body is stationary. One foot is kept in contact with the surface area, while the other foot is used to push off. A turn is made in the desired direction with the weight on the foot that has maintained contact with the surface area. The angle of the pivot (turn) is determined by the need in the particular situation. The angle is not likely to be over 180 degrees, as might be the case in pivoting away from an opponent in basketball.

Theoretically, the pivot is executed on only one foot. However, a *reverse turn* is sometimes referred to as a "two-foot" pivot. In this case, a complete turn to the opposite direction is made with both feet on the surface area. With one foot ahead of the other, the heels are raised, and a turn is made with weight equally distributed on both feet.

Pivoting is important in the performance of many kinds of sports activities where quick movements are necessary while the body remains stationary. This is particularly true in games like basketball where a limited number of steps can be taken while in possession of the ball.

Some Ways Children Can Practice Pivoting

1. With a partner, pivot when he or she calls out a signal.
2. Face your partner and practice pivoting away from him or her.
3. Run to a point, stop and pivot, and then run back.

4. Have a partner throw a ball to you. When you catch it, make a pivot and protect the ball.
5. Pivot on one foot and then the other. Do this several times.

Landing

Landing is concerned with the body coming to the surface area from a height or distance. Absorption when landing is accomplished by bending the knees. The weight is on the balls of the feet, and there is flexion at the ankle and knee joints. After landing, the performer comes to an upright position with the arms in a sideward position so as to keep the body in balance.

Many games such as basketball, volleyball, and football require the performer to leave the surface area, which makes the skill of landing important. In addition, vaulting over objects in apparatus activities requires skill in landing, not only for good performance but for safety as well.

Some Ways Children Can Practice Landing

1. Take a short jump into the air and land – remember how landing was explained above.
2. Jump into the air and land; repeat this several time.
3. Take a short slow run, jump, and land.
4. Jump from a short height such as a bench or a chair.

Falling

In those activities that require staying in an upright position, emphasis, of course, should be on maintaining this position. Nevertheless, there are occasions when a performer loses balance and falls to the surface area. Whenever possible, a fall should be taken in such a way that injury is least likely to occur. One way to accomplish this is to attempt to "break the fall" with the hands. Relaxation and flexion at the joints that put the performer in a "bunched" position are helpful in avoiding injury when falling to the surface area.

Some Ways Children Can Practice Falling

1. Find a soft place and roll around in a curled up position.
2. Pretend you are a ball and roll around on a soft place.
3. Pretend you are a leaf falling slowly from a tree.
4. Pretend you are a melting snowman.

SKILLS OF PROPULSION AND RETRIEVAL

Skills which involve propelling and retrieving objects, in most cases a ball, are used in many types of games. It is the purpose of this section of the chapter to provide the reader with knowledge which is important to an understanding of such propelling and retrieving skills as throwing, striking, kicking and catching.

Throwing

The skill of throwing involves the release of a ball with one or both hands. In general, there are three factors concerned with success in throwing. These are the accuracy or direction of the throw, the distance which the ball must be thrown and the amount of force needed to propel the ball.

Any release of an object from the hand or hands could be considered an act of throwing. With this definition in mind, the average infant of six months is able to perform a reasonable facsimile of throwing from a sitting position. It has been estimated that by four years of age, about 20 percent of the children show at least a degree of proficiency in throwing. This ability tends to increase rapidly, and between the ages of five or six, over three-fourths of the children can attain a reasonable degree of proficiency as previously defined here.

Gender differences in the early throwing behavior of children tend to favor boys. At all age levels, boys are generally superior to girls in throwing for distance. However, there is not such a profound gender difference in throwing for accuracy.

There are generally three accepted throwing patterns. These are (1) the underarm pattern, (2) the sidearm pattern and (3) the overarm pattern. It should be noticed that although the ball is released by one or both hands, the term "arm" is used in connection with the various patterns. The reason is that the patterns involve a "swing" of the arm.

Underarm Throwing Pattern

The child ordinarily begins the underarm throwing pattern by releasing the ball from both hands. However, the child is soon able to release with one hand, especially when the ball is small enough to grip.

At the starting position, the thrower stands facing in the direction of the throw. The feet should be in a parallel position and slightly apart. The right arm is in a position nearly perpendicular to the surface area. (All of the descriptions involving the skills of propulsion and retrieval are for the right-handed child. In the case of the left-handed child, just the opposite should apply.) To start the throw, the right arm is brought back (back swing) to a position where it is about parallel with the surface area. Simultaneously, there is a slight rotation of the body to the right with most of the weight transferred to the right foot. As the arm comes forward (front swing) a step is taken with the left foot. (Stepping out with the opposite foot of the swinging arm is known as the *principle of opposition*.) The ball is released on the front swing when the arm is about parallel to the surface area. During the process of the arm swing, the arm is straight, prescribing a semicircle with no flexion at the elbow. The right foot is carried forward as a part of the follow through after the release.

The underarm throwing pattern is used in games that involve passing the ball from one person to another over a short distance. It is also used for pitching in softball.

Sidearm Throwing Pattern

Aside from the direction the thrower faces and the plane of the arm swing, the mechanical principles applied in the sidearm throwing pattern are essentially the same as the underarm throwing pattern.

The thrower faces at a right angle to the direction of the throw, whereas in the underarm throwing pattern he or she faces in the direction of the throw. The arm is brought to the back swing in a horizontal plane or a position parallel to the surface area. Body rotation and weight shift is the same as in the underarm pattern. The arm remains straight and a semicircle is prescribed from the back swing to the release of the ball on the front swing.

The sidearm throwing pattern will ordinarily be used to propel a ball that is too large to grip with one hand. Thus on the back swing the opposite hand helps control the ball until there is sufficient momentum during the swing. Greater distance can be obtained with the sidearm throwing pattern with a ball too large to grip, but accuracy is more difficult to maintain.

Overarm Throwing Pattern

Again the basic body mechanics of the overarm throwing pattern are essentially the same as the two previous patterns. The thrower faces in the same direction as for the sidearm throwing pattern; that is, at a right angle to the direction of the throw. Depending upon individual differences this position may vary. An essential difference in the overarm throwing pattern is the position of the arm. Whereas, in the two previous patterns the arm was kept straight, in the overarm throwing pattern there is flexion at the elbow. Thus, on the back swing the arm is brought back with the elbow bent and with the arm at a right angle away from the body. The arm is then brought forward and the ball is released in a "whip-like" motion at about the height of the shoulder. Foot and arm follow through is the same as with the underarm and sidearm throwing patterns. This pattern is used for throwing a ball that can be gripped with the fingers in such games as baseball where distance as well as accuracy are important.

Striking

Striking involves propelling a ball with a part of the body, ordinarily the hand, as in handball or with an implement such as a bat in baseball. The object to be struck can be stationary; that is, batting a ball from a batting tee or moving such as a pitched ball in baseball.

As early as age three, verbal direction to children will educe a sidearm striking pattern with a plastic paddle when a tennis ball is suspended in a stationary position at about waist high. Also at the same age, the child will have a degree of success with the sidearm striking pattern when a light ball is tossed to him or her.

The principles of body mechanics and the striking patterns are essentially the same as the three previously mentioned throwing patterns – underarm, sidearm, and overarm. The same movements are applied, but in order to propel an object by striking, greater speed is needed with the striking movement. For example, greater speed of movement is needed in the underarm striking pattern when serving a volleyball, that in releasing a ball with a short toss in the underarm throw.

Kicking

Kicking involves propelling a ball with either foot. As early as age two the average child is able to maintain balance on one foot and propel a stationary ball with the other foot. At this early age the child is likely to have limited action of the kicking foot with little or no follow through. With advancing age, better balance and strength is maintained and by age six, the child can develop a full leg back swing and a body lean into the kick of a stationary ball.

In kicking, contact with the ball is made with the (1) inside of the foot, (2) outside of the foot, or (3) with the instep of the foot. With the exception of these positions of the foot the mechanical principles of kicking are essentially the same. The kicking leg is swung back with flexion at the knee. The leg swings forward with the foot making contact with the ball. As in the case of the skill of striking, contact with the ball in kicking can be made when the ball is either stationary or moving.

There is not complete agreement in terms of progression in which the skill of kicking is learned. On the basis of personal experience, we recommend the following sequence.

Stationary

The ball and the kicker remain stationary, and the kicker stands beside the ball and kicks it. The kicker is concerned only with the leg movement, and it is more likely that the head will be kept down with the eyes on the ball at the point of contact.

Stationary and Run

This means that the ball is in a stationary position and that the kicker takes a short run up to the ball before kicking it. This is more difficult, as the kicker must time and coordinate the run to make proper contact with the ball.

Kick from Hands

This is referred to as "punting," as in football or soccer. The ball is dropped from the hands of the kicker who takes one or two steps and kicks the ball as it drops. The child is kicking a moving ball, but has control over the movement of the ball before kicking it.

Kicking a Moving Ball

Another person could pitch or roll the ball to the kicker as in the game of kickball. This is perhaps the most difficult kick because the kicker must kick a moving ball that is or has been under the control of another person, as in the case of a ground ball in soccer.

Catching

When we think of visual perception, we are concerned about "keeping your eye on the ball" and "looking the ball into your hands." This involves *tracking* which is the ability to maintain focus on a moving object. The importance of tracking in catching should be obvious.

Tracking patterns can vary according to whether the ball is moving through the air or along the ground. It is usually easier to track a moving ball on the ground as more environmental cues are available. The position of the ball in relation to the ground and other objects can be used to help predict its final position. The eyes focus on the ball prior to, and at release, to determine the velocity and direction it will travel. The catcher then follows the path intermittently. That is, the eyes do not maintain a steadfast focus on the ball. The catcher should be able to look at the ball and predict its future position in an ongoing manner. This intermittent monitoring allows the processing of other relevant information. This is especially important in many high skill level team games where the environment can be unpredictable; that is, movement of other players on the playing area.

Catching with the hands is the most frequently used retrieving skill. One of the child's first experiences with catching occurs at an early stage in life, as when he or she sits with the legs in a spread position and another person rolls a ball to the child. By four years of age, about one-third of the children can retrieve a ball in aerial flight thrown from a short distance. Slightly over one-half can perform this feat by age five, and about two-thirds of them can accomplish this by age six.

There are certain basic mechanical principles that should be taken into account in the skill of catching. It is of importance that the catcher position himself or herself as nearly "in line" with the ball as possible. In this position, the child will be better able to receive the ball near the center of gravity of the body. Another important factor is hand position. A ball will approach the catcher (1) at the waist, (2) above the waist, or (3) below the waist. When the ball approaches about the waist level, the palms should be facing each other with fingers pointing straight ahead. The "heels" of the hands should be close together depending upon the size of the ball; that is, closer for a small ball and farther apart for a large ball. When the ball approaches above the waist, the palms face the ball and the fingers point upward with the thumbs as close together as necessary. When the ball approaches below the waist the palms still face the ball but the fingers face downward with the little fingers as close together as seems necessary. When the ball reaches the hands, it is brought in towards the body; that is, the catcher "gives" with the catch in order to control the ball and absorb the shock. The position of the feet will likely depend upon the speed with which the ball approaches. Ordinarily, one foot should be in advance of the other in a stride position, with the distance determined by the speed of the approaching ball.

The above discussion has been concerned only with retrieving a ball with both hands. Let us examine the skill of catching a ball with one hand.

Most of the research conducted on catching has been that of two-handed catching. An interesting study was conducted by Fischman, Moore, and Steele,[1] the primary purpose of which was to begin to describe the development of simple one-hand catching of young children.

The investigation involved 240 children, ranging in age, as of their 1st birthday, from 5 to 12 years (120 boys and 120 girls). Within each of the eight groups, 15 boys and 15 girls were observed.

The children were asked to use their preferred hand to catch a total of 24 tennis balls, tossed underarm by an experimenter, from a distance of nine feet. Hand preference was ascertained by asking the children to show which hand they used for brushing their teeth. Of the 240 children, 208 used their right hand and 32 used their left hand.

The nine-foot distance was selected because pilot work indicated that this distance could be used to adequately discriminate between the youngest and oldest children, while proving neither too difficult and frustrating for the 5-year-olds nor too easy for the 12-year-olds. A subject sample was desired that could successfully catch with two hands, especially in the younger age group, and the pilot work showed that nine-foot distance did produce successful two-hand catching.

Four different locations were designated as the targets for the tosses: (1) Waist height, (2) shoulder height, (3) above-the-head, and (4) out-to-the-side, at about waist height. For the first three locations, an attempt was made to place the toss approximately even with the catching arm. For the fourth location, the ball was tossed so that the subjects had to reach out to the side for it but could do so without changing their body position. All balls were tossed at a moderate pace. For the waist and out-to-the-side locations, tosses were made with a slight arc so that the ball was moving downward when the catch was completed. These trajectories were adjusted slightly to accommodate the subject's height.

Results revealed that catching performance improved with age, boys caught more balls than girls, ball location influenced catching success, and in general, the location of the toss contained the child's selection of an appropriate hand-arm orientation. With the possible exception of the shoulder location for girls, even very young children are sensitive to the perceptual aspects of the toss and respond with an appropriate orientation.

There are few instances where a child uses the one-hand catch in sports activities. An exception, of course, is in baseball, but the catch is made easier with the use of a glove.

In closing this chapter, we want to state that it should be obvious that how well a child is able to perform certain basic skills is directly related to the success he or she will have in a sport requiring those skills. For this reason care should be taken to see that children are well prepared in skill performance. To a large extent this ability will be a factor in the type of sport a child will be able to engage in successfully. Unfortunately, some children are pressured into certain sports by parents at too early an age before the child is ready for the skill levels required in those sports.

ENDNOTE

1. Fischman, Mark G., Moore, Jane B., and Steele, Kenneth H., Children's One-Hand Catching as a Function of Age, Gender, and Ball Location, *Research Quarterly for Exercise and Sports*, December 1992.

Chapter 4

FOOTBALL

In the United States the word *football* generally refers only to the American game; in other nations of the world it usually means soccer. Most of the modern forms of football are derived from the ancient games, especially *harpaston* and *harpastrum*, played in Greece and Rome. These games were carried over through the Middle Ages down to present times in Tuscany and Florence under the name of *calcio*. Meanwhile a rugged undisciplined type of football took root in England in the Middle Ages, and despite several edicts banning the game from time to time, football remained popular among the masses until the 19th century. Different forms of the game were soon developed at the various English public schools – at Eton, Rugby, Harrow and others. Eventually two main games emerged. One was primarily a kicking game, which later became association football, or soccer; the other (dating from 1823) was football as played at the Rugby School, in which carrying the ball and tackling were permitted. It was from the two English games, especially rugby, that American football developed.[1]

The American game is played by two opposing teams of 11 players each. (In some high schools with a small enrollment, a team consists of six or eight players.) The field is level and is 100 yards long and 530 yards wide. It is marked off by latitudinal stripes every five yards and is flanked on each end by an endzone 10 yards deep. In each endzone stands H-shaped goal posts not exceeding 20 feet in height, with the crossbar 10 feet from the ground and with the vertical posts 24 feet apart. (The dimensions of the playing field may be modified for younger players.) Play is directed toward gaining possession of the football – an inflated, almost egg-shaped leather ball – and moving it across the opponent's goal line, thereby scoring a touchdown, worth six points. In advancing the ball a team may run or pass (forward or laterally), but it must gain 10 yards in four tries (or downs), or else yield possession of the ball to the opponent. The defending team tries to stop the ball carrier from advancing by tackling him; that is forcing him to the ground – thus causing the team with the ball to use one of its downs. The defending team can gain possession of the ball before the end of four downs by recovering a dropped ball (fumble), or by intercepting a pass. Because of the strategies and skills required, most organized football teams have offensive and defensive squads that alternate on the field as possession of the ball changes.

In addition to the touchdown, points are scored by kicking the ball over the crossbar between the goal posts (field goal) counting three points; and by downing a player in possession of the ball behind his own goal line (a safety), counting two points. Additional points, known as conversions (extra points), may be scored after completion of a touchdown. In professional play the conversion is worth one point and is earned by kicking the ball over the goal line from two yards, or two points by running or passing the ball over the goal line from two yards away. In amateur (high school and college) football, where the conversion play is begun three yards away from the goal line, the kick is worth one point and the running or passing conversion, two points. When a team is not likely to gain 10 yards in four downs, it often kicks, or punts the ball downfield, usually on fourth down. After each down before resuming play, the opposing teams face each other along an imaginary line of scrimmage, determined by the position of the ball on the field of play.

Blocking and tackling make football one of the most rugged sports played; thus, football players wear heavy protective gear. (The rugged play, viewed by some as rather violent, is a reason often given by parents for not permitting their children to play the game.) Indeed, the frequency of reported serious injury and deaths in middle school, high school and college football is of considerable concern to parents as well as to those who research sport injuries.

Although participation in football (particularly "tackle" football) by children is a controversial issue among some parents, it is a popular sport among many children. In our surveys football rated high among boys as the game they "liked to play best" also, there appears to be an increasing interest in the game among girls – particularly the type of football games that do not involve tackling.

According to our interviews with parents, coaches, professional players and children themselves, there is little or no agreement on the age at which children should be allowed to participate in the "tackle" version of football. One school of thought is reflected in the belief of one coach who has coached Boys Club 8-9-year-olds for seven years. His feeling is that at that age level they are not "big enough or strong enough to knock each other around." He maintained that in his seven-year tenure there were no serious injuries incurred by his or opposing players.

Conversely, many professional football players seem to prefer that their own children wait to participate until they are at least of high school age. The reason given by many of these professionals is essentially the same as that of most educators who feel that the contact in football can be harmful to the development of growing children. In fact, a quarterback who played in the National Football League for 10 years indicated that he had to "fight off" his own son's participation until he was 13 years of age. He said he was forced to relent because of his child's loss of status among his peers.

Others pointed out that children will play football on their own anyway so their thinking is "why not be organized with proper equipment if appropriate supervision is provided."

There is no question about it; this is not an easy problem to resolve. As stated previously, adults should thoroughly explore the type of supervision that will be available to assure the safety and well being of the child who prefers to participate. Parents should resist the temptation to relive their own lives through their own children – particularly those fathers who were themselves "frustrated athletes." Moreover, it is doubtful that there is any reason why a child should be *pressured* into participating in any sport if he or she desires not to do so.

FOOTBALL SKILLS

There are a number of skills that need to be acquired if one is to have success in football. Each skill is important, while some might be more important to the individual player, depending on the role/position which he or she plays in the game.

Passing

An important thing to remember in football skills is the shape of the ball. In all other games the ball is round. And, of course, the balls come in different sizes as we can see when we compare a basketball and a baseball. Because the ball is oval shaped in football some of the skills may be more difficult to perform. There are two kinds of passes in football, the *forward* pass and the *lateral* pass.

Forward Pass

The first thing to think about in forward passing is how to grip the ball. The fingers of the throwing hand grip the lace behind the center of the ball. The fingers are spread over the laces and the thumb around the ball. The smaller the hand, the nearer the end of the ball it should be.

The pass is made with the overarm throwing pattern which was explained in Chapter 3. A right-handed thrower can use the left hand to help hold the ball while gripping it with the right hand. The ball is brought back past the ear. The body turns a little away from the direction of the throw. There is a step forward with the left foot pointing in the direction of the target. The weight shifts from the right to the left foot. The elbow of the throwing arm moves forward. The forearm comes forward with a whipping action with the ball rolling off the finger tips. The ball should be thrown a little ahead of the person who is to catch it. This is the receiver who will be moving – or directly toward the mid-section to upper mid-section of the receiver who is stationary. Here are some important things to remember when throwing a forward pass.

1. Be sure to point the left foot in the direction of the throw if the thrower is right-handed. If left-handed, the right foot will be pointed in the direction of the throw.
2. Grip the ball where it is most comfortable. The thrower may have to grip it nearer the end if he has a small hand.

3. Keep the eyes on the target; that is, the person who is to catch the ball.
4. Practice to see how far back past the ear you will need to bring the ball.
5. Let the ball off the fingers with a whipping motion.
6. Follow through and have the fingers pointing generally towards the target at the end of the throw.

Lateral Pass

A lateral pass is one that is thrown sideways. It can be done with one or both hands. When done with one hand, it is about the same as the underarm throwing pattern. The one-handed lateral pass is not used much by young players because the ball is difficult to grip.

When throwing a two-handed lateral pass, the player gets a firm grip on the ball with both hands. The player may be running with the ball prior to the time to lateral (as in the case of the run/lateral option play). The ball is usually gripped with both hands. The ball is then shifted to the side of the body opposite the throw. The player brings the ball across the body and releases it about waist high. Sometimes the quicker laterals (usually by older, more experienced players) will be executed with one hand and/or done with a more rapid "flipping" motion from in front of side of the player doing the lateral.

In football, catching is thought of as *receiving*. Sometimes the ball will not get to the receiver. When that happens he must stop and wait for the ball.

One foot is slightly ahead of the other. The feet are spread in a comfortable position. The arms and hands are extended toward the person who is passing the ball. The fingers are spread, and the hands are made into a cup.

As the ball comes toward the receiver, the weight is transferred to the foot that steps toward the ball. If the pass is high, the arms and hands move upward. The hands form a cup. When the ball is thrown low, the arms and hands are downward. The little fingers are together, and the hands again form a cup. The receiver "gives" with the ball when he contacts it. After the ball is caught, one end of it is placed under the arm above the elbow. The other hand is over the other end of the ball, and the player is now in a position to run with the ball.

Catching a Pass

Catching a forward pass is a very difficult skill. Because the receiver ordinarily catches it while running, this kind of pass requires good timing and balance.

The reader should consider again the skill of running as explained in Chapter 3. After good running skill is developed, the receiver is better prepared to catch a forward pass.

The body weight is forward in the running position as the ball come in. The arms and hands move upward to make the catch. The receiver looks over his shoulder at the passer and/or the ball. The arms and fingers are extended above the shoulders. The palms of the hands face the ball. The little fingers are together, and the hands form a cup. When the receiver gets control of the ball, he brings it down to carrying position. One end of the ball is placed above the elbow under the arm and the hand over the end of the ball. Often the receiver will protect the ball by covering it with the other hand and arm, especially just prior to being hit or tackled in order to keep from dropping the ball.

Catching a Kicked Ball

There are two conditions when a player may be required to catch a kicked ball. One of these is when a ball is kicked off to start the game or after a score. The other is when the ball is punted by the other team. When a ball is kicked off, it will usually come in end over end. When it is punted, it will probably come in as a spiral, as in a forward pass. (However, a punt could come in end over end if it has not been punted well.) Even though the kicked ball can approach in either of these ways, the way to catch it is about the same.

The player should try to get into a position where he thinks the ball will come down. This means trying to get lined up with the ball. The hands and arms are extended outward to form a "basket," making sure the weight is even on both feet. In the catching action, the fingers are spread apart forming a cup. The palms are upward. When contact is made with the ball the player gives with the hands and arms. The ball is pulled toward the middle of the body. As soon as there is control of the ball, it is placed under the arm and the player starts running.

Carrying the Ball

In running with the ball the ball carrier leans forward applying his best running skill. One end of the ball is placed under the arm and next to the body. There is a firm grip over the other end of the ball. This means that the player makes a cradle with the arm so that the ball will not fall out. When starting to run with the ball, short steps are taken. Knees are kept high to be able to change direction. Remember the skill of dodging explained in Chapter 3. It is very important for a ball carrier to be able to dodge well. When carrying the ball in an open field, longer strides are taken to get more speed. The ball should be carried in the arm that is nearest the sideline. This can help to prevent the ball from being lost (fumbled) when the ball carrier is tackled.

Centering the Ball

Centering the ball is the way a play is started in football. The player who is the center passes or "hikes" the ball to: (1) the quarterback up close in the T or other formation, (2) to the quarterback set back farther in the shotgun formation, (3) to another player in the backfield, or (4) to the place-kicker holder or punter.

In the starting position the center crouches down over the ball. The legs are spread, and one foot is a little bit behind the other. The knees are bent and the weight is even on both feet. The right hand is placed over the front half of the ball. The left hand is on the back half of the ball. The thumbs are on top, and the fingers are on the side. The hips are about even with the shoulders.

In centering the ball to the quarterback in the T formation the ball is handed to him with one hand. In centering under conditions 3 and 4 above, just before centering the ball, the body weight moves forward toward the toes. Very little weight is on the ball. The ball is passed back with both hands between the legs. The right hand passes the ball, and the left hand guides it.

After the ball is let go, the center steps forward with the back foot. He is then ready to move forward.

Punting

In the starting position the kicker stands with the weight on the back foot. The arms are out in front, and both hands hold the ball. The left hand is on the left side of the ball near the front. The right hand is on the right side of the ball near the back. The front part of the ball is turned a little to the left.

There is a step forward with the left foot. Next there is a step with the right foot. Then there is another step with the left foot. The arms and ball stay in the same position during the steps. The eyes are kept on the ball. Remember that the body weight is on the foot *not* used for kicking. If the kicker is right footed, the weight is on the left foot.

When the kicking leg comes forward, the ball is let go with both hands. The ball is kicked with the top of the foot. The toes are pointed in the direction of the kick.

Place Kicking

The reader should refer back to the description of the "Stationary and Run" kick in Chapter 3. Most place kickers use what is called the "soccer style" kick. The kicker approaches the ball from an angle rather than head on. The kick is made with the instep with the toe pointed down and to the outer edge of the ball.

Stance

Stance means the position a player takes before play starts. This starting position can be either a three-point stance or a four-point stance. (Sometimes players in the backfield will take a stance with their hands resting on their knees.)

In the three-point stance the feet are about shoulder width apart. One foot is slightly ahead of the other. The player takes a crouch position with the knees bent. The weight is slightly forward and resting mostly on the knuckles of one hand. The reason it is called a three-point stance is that the player is on both feet and the knuckles of one hand. The head should be up with the eyes looking straight ahead. A player can move very quickly from this position.

In the four-point stance, the weight is on both feet and the knuckles of both hands. Everything else is the same as the three-point stance, and either of these stances can be used. The stance chosen depends upon the position one is playing; that is, the line or backfield. Usually the backfield and linemen will use the three-point stance on offense. The four-point stance is used mainly by linemen on defense. The most important issue, of course, is to get into the stance that is most comfortable.

Blocking and Tackling

Blocking in football means that the player gets his body in front of a player on the other team. He tries to block his path and engage him in contact so his opponent cannot get to the ball carrier. For the most part, the shoulders and hips are used in blocking. Use of the hands in blocking can sometimes be interpreted as "holding" and this is cause for a penalty.

Tackling means that one or more players bring the opposing ball carrier to the ground. A defensive player may take hold of the ball carrier on any part of the body. However, it is a penalty to take hold of the ball carrier's face mask because this can result in serious injury.

TEAM PLAY

There are several things to keep in mind in offensive and defensive play in football. The following are some of the things for a player to remember about offensive play.

1. A player should know what he specifically is supposed to do on each play.

2. Do not give the play away. Use the same stance each time when lining up.
3. Remember the right carrying position when carrying the ball.
4. Practice the skill of dodging so as to be better at carrying the ball.
5. A receiver should use both hands to catch a ball.

The following are some things to remember about defensive play.

1. When defending against a pass receiver, keep in front of him. It might be a good idea to practice the skill of galloping both forward and backward. This practice can help a player change direction quickly when defending against a receiver. The skill of galloping was explained in Chapter 3.
2. Watch the ball and try to intercept it or tip it away from the receiver before he can catch it.
3. A lineman should keep his eyes on the ball. Watching the ball will help to follow the person carrying the ball.
4. In defending against a pass, the player must try to watch both the passer and the ball.
5. When the passer lets the ball go, watch the ball and follow it.

FLAG FOOTBALL

Flag football grew out of the game of touch football. The game of touch football grew out of the game of American football. Many people did not have a chance to engage in the game of football. The reason was that it was a very expensive game to play. So much equipment was needed that the average person did not have enough money to pay for it. Touch football provided a game where all could play without much expense.

The big difference in the game of touch football and regular football is that in touch football tackling is not allowed. This makes the game of touch football much less dangerous to play. In touch football a player is stopped by being touched rather than by being tackled. Because touching sometimes resulted in a form of pushing, which could cause serious injury, flag football was introduced. This game is the same as touch football except that a cloth (flag) is tucked in at the back of the waist of a player. A player is stopped when an opponent pulls the flag loose from the waist. This action is likely to prevent injury, and at the same time there is little question that the person with the ball was stopped. For these reasons the game of flag football is used in many schools, especially in intramural programs.

GAMES TO PRACTICE FOOTBALL SKILLS

The following games are useful to help players develop certain football skills. These games can be used as practice drills. They can also be used as substitute activities for the more highly complex game of football for those children who are not ready or do not prefer to play the game of football.

Football Keep Away

Two or more teams with any number of players can play this game. Play starts with one of the teams having the ball. This team passes the ball around to its own players. The other team(s) try to get the ball. When one of the teams intercepts the ball, that team gets it and tries to pass it around and keep it from the other teams. This game helps players develop the skill of handling the oval-shaped football.

Leader Ball Center Relay

Four or more players can play this game. One player is selected to be the leader and stands with his or her back to the other players, who are standing in a line. The leader centers the ball to each member of the group. They return the ball to the leader. When a player misses the ball, he or she goes to the foot of the line. If the leader misses, he or she goes to the foot of the line, and the player at the head of the line replaces the leader. If desired, there can be several groups playing the game at the same time. The idea of this game is to practice the skill of centering and catching the ball.

Football Kickball

This game requires two teams with any number on each team. The game is played on a baseball diamond. All of the rules of softball are used. The ball is kicked instead of batted. The kicker stands at home plate and punts the ball. He runs to first base if the ball lands fair. All other rules of softball are used for the game. The idea of the game is to practice punting and catching punts but at the same time make a game of it.

Football Zig-Zag

There are two teams of any number of players. Each team forms a line that faces the other team. The player at one end of the line starts the game by passing to a teammate across from him. The player passes the ball back and so on. The game goes on until the ball gets to the last player in the line. The first team to get the ball back to the leader wins. The purpose of this game is to practice the skill of forward passing, and catching as well.

Teacher Football

Any number can play this game. It is probably best not to have more than five or six players. In this way the game goes faster, and the players get more turns. One player is selected to be the "teacher." The other players form a line facing the teacher. The teacher passes the ball to anyone in the line. If the player drops the ball, he goes to the end of the line, and the rest of the players move up. If the teacher drops the ball he goes to the end of the line, and the player at the beginning of the line becomes the teacher.

Kick and Catch

Two teams are needed for this game. There can be any number on each team. One team stands at one side of the field, and the other team stands at the other side. The game starts with the player of one team punting the ball to the other team. The player on the other team who is closest to the ball tries to catch it. If he catches it he kicks it back. If the player misses the catch, the other team scores a point. After a certain amount of time, the team with the most points wins the game. This game gives players a chance to practice the skill of punting and also the skill of catching a kicked ball.

The game of football as we know it in the United States has grown greatly in popularity over the previous four decades and today is played widely by youth teams all the way up through professional ranks. The size, speed, and aggressiveness of players have increased. Also, the overall effectiveness and protective quality of the gear/equipment has improved over this period.

ENDNOTE

1. The Columbia Encyclopedia, Columbia University Press, sixth edition, 2000, p. 1012, Ed. Paul Lagasse.

Chapter 5

BASEBALL

A form of baseball, probably derived from the English games of cricket and rounders was played in the 19th century and the children's game of *One Old Cat* probably existed before that. This original game is played as follows: there are only two bases, first base and home base. As many as desired can be on each team. The first batter fungo bats the ball and runs to first base and back. A complete trip must be made. If the batter makes a complete trip without being put out, a run is scored for that team. The runner is out if a fly ball is caught or a fielder touches the runner with the ball before the runner reaches home. When a team makes three outs they change places. (Fungo batting means that the batter throws the ball up and hits it.) For a right-handed batter, the bat is held with the right hand. It can rest on the shoulder, or it can be held out to the side. The ball is held in the left hand. The weight is on the back foot. A step is taken to the side with the left foot. The ball is tossed up high enough to give time to get the left hand on the bat for the swing. Although the game One Old Cat is still played, interest in it has diminished over the years.

Baseball was played mostly in the northeastern states before the Civil War. About 1845, Alexander Cartwright set bases at about 90 feet apart. A commission headed by A. G. Mills issued a report that declared that Abner Doubleday created the modern game in 1839 at Cooperstown, New York. However, it is interesting to note that this has been refuted by some authorities.[1] In fact, it was recently discovered that the game could have been played more than a decade before 1839. In the fall of the year 2000 two newspaper articles which appeared on April 25, 1823 were discovered by George A. Thompson, Jr. a librarian at New York University. The articles described the activity as the "manly exercise of baseball."[2]

In the early days players caught the ball with their bare hands. This became so hard on the hands that players began to use a baseball glove. The man who made baseball gloves popular was Albert Goodwill Spaulding. He was a great pitcher for the Chicago White Stockings (now White Sox), and he started wearing a black leather glove in 1877 when he played first base. Catching a ball became easier as gloves were made larger. Today's gloves are more than twice the size as they were originally.[3]

When we think of children's baseball, the name *Little League* immediately comes to mind. Started in 1939, the league was originally for players 9 to 12 years of age. Little League Baseball is played on a 60 foot diamond with 46 feet from the pitching mound to the home plate. Eight-year-olds and others with less experience can play in what is called the *Minor League*. For younger children (5-8 years old) *Tee Ball* is used to help children learn the fundamentals of hitting and fielding. In Tee Ball, players hit a ball of a batting tee. Rules of the game may be varied to accommodate the need for teaching. The primary goals of Tee Ball are to instruct children in the fundamentals of baseball and to allow them to experience the value of teamwork. (Incidentally, a game of Tee Ball was played on the south lawn of the White House on May 6, 2001. Public reaction to this event has been mixed with some saying it was simply politically motivated and others say it was carried out for the purpose of rejuvenating a waning interest in the game of baseball.)

In addition to Little League Baseball some of the other children's baseball leagues are Babe Ruth, Pony Baseball, and Dixie Baseball. Some leagues make an effort to modify the game by rotating rosters every week or two so there are no team standings. In some leagues, no scores are kept in Tee Ball or "Coach-Pitch Leagues." In many leagues every player must play; in some, every player must play in the infield at least some of the time.

BASEBALL SKILLS

The most important skills in baseball are throwing, catching, batting, and running. As mentioned before, running is a skill used in most games. In baseball it is used to run and field the ball and to run around the bases. The skills of catching, throwing, and batting in baseball are not easy to learn. One of the reasons for this is that players use a much smaller ball than they do in many other games. This sometimes makes the ball difficult to control.

Throwing

The skills of throwing and the patterns of throwing were explained in Chapter 3. The reader should refer back to that chapter to review these skills. Sometimes the underarm throw is used as a short toss when a ball is fielded close to a base; for example, when it is fielded too close to use the overarm throwing pattern.

Catching

Catching in baseball is done largely the same as was explained in Chapter 3. However, the ball is smaller and might be harder to control. It is a good idea first to practice catching balls that are thrown than to catch a ball that is batted.

Fielding

Catching or stopping a ball after it has been hit by a batter is called fielding. When the ball comes to the player through the air it is called a fly ball. When it comes along the ground it is called a ground ball or a grounder.

Fielding Fly Balls

It is important to get lined up with the ball in fielding a fly ball because the ball comes in with such force. The fielder should keep his or her eyes on the ball. As soon as the ball leaves the bat the fielder should track it with the eyes. The ball is watched closely as it comes through the air and then the fielder gets ready to catch it. When the ball is high the player should try to catch it above the chin. The thumbs are together with the fingers pointing upward. When the ball drops low the player should try to catch it near the waist. The little fingers are close together. On either a high ball or low ball the player makes a little basket by spreading the cupping fingers. The body leans forward with the arms bent. The weight is placed evenly on both feet. If the player runs up to the ball the weight is shifted to the front foot when catching it. The bare hand follows the ball into the glove to hold the ball.

Fielding fly balls is not an easy skill, and sometimes young players may make mistakes such as the following:

1. Not lining up with the ball.
2. Running up too soon to meet the ball and thus over-running it.
3. Not running up soon enough to meet the ball.
4. Catching the ball with the hand in front of the eyes. When this is done the player can drop the ball because of taking the eyes off of it.
5. Trying to catch the ball with one hand under it and the other hand over it. The hands should be side by side.
6. Not giving with the ball. If this is not done, the ball may hit the glove and bounce out.

Fielding Ground Balls

Again it is important to get in line with the ball. For a right-handed player the left foot should be forward. The body bends at the hips, knees and ankles, trying to keep the upper part of the body straight. The fingers point downward and the hands are placed just opposite the left foot. The player then tries to contact the ball just inside the left foot with the left hand. The ball is contacted with the right hand so that the player can get control of it. As soon as the player fields the ball he or she is in a position to raise the body for the throw.

Pitching

Pitching in baseball is done with the overarm throwing pattern which was explained in Chapter 3. The following are some important things for a pitcher to remember.

1. Step toward the batter when letting the ball go.
2. Aim at target.
3. Follow through with the pitching arm.
4. At the end of the pitch, the fingers point toward the target.
5. The target is about three feet above home plate.
6. Work together with the catcher.

Batting

Batting is a striking skill and was explained in Chapter 3. One of the first things about batting is how to grip the bat. If a player is right handed, the left hand is wrapped around the bat about two or three inches from the end. The right hand is wrapped around the bat just above the left hand. If the bat is heavy, or if it is a long bat, the player can wrap the left hand around much higher on the bat. This is called the "choke" grip. A bat should be swung several times to make sure the player is gripping it in a way that feels best.

A right-handed batter stands with the left side of the body facing the pitcher. The feet are parallel and about shoulder-width apart. The bat is held back of the head. It is about shoulder high. The arms are bent at the elbows and are held away from the body. When the ball leaves the pitcher's hand, the batter's weight should be shifted to the rear foot. If the batter decides to strike at the ball, he or she swings the bat forward, level with the ground. The weight is shifted to the left foot. The trade mark (printing on the bat) should be facing the batter.

Bunting

Bunting is a form of batting used to hit a ball a very short distance. Bunting can be done to surprise the fielders. It is usually done by very fast runners. They need to have a lot of speed in order to get to first base before the bunt is fielded.

In bunting, the batter should stand straight. The feet are apart so that the player can get the bat in front of the ball anywhere in the "strike zone." The left hand stays in the same place on the bat. The right hand slides abut halfway up the bat. There is no swing at the ball; it just hits the bat.

Baserunning

The skill of running as described in Chapter 3 applies much the same to baserunning. The main difference is that the runner will run only 60 feet in a straight line (the distance between bases). This distance is sometimes shortened for boys and girls at certain ages.

As soon as the ball is hit, the bat is dropped safely and the runner starts the run to first base. If the runner sees that he or she may only be able to get to first base, it is best to run "through" the base. If the runner decides that he or she can get more than one base, there may be a try for second base. In this case, the runner curves out to the right a few feet before reaching first base. In order to curve out the runner must slow down the run. The foot touches the inside of the base so that the runner will not run wide at the base. When the baserunner is waiting on base he or she leans forward with the left foot on the base. The runner can "lead off" a few feet if so desired.

PLAYING THE DIFFERENT POSITIONS

In just about every team sport most members of both teams are all active at the same time. This is not the case in baseball. The batting team has one player at bat. It can have no more than three players on base. This means that at any one time the *offensive* team can have as many as four players and as few as one player active.

The fielding team or *defensive* team has nine of its players ready for action. At least they should be. Many times beginners in the game of baseball do not do well because they are not sure what they are supposed to do in their positions. The following are some suggestions of some of the things each player is supposed to do in the various positions.

Catcher

1. Stands behind the batter in a knee bend position.
2. Holds the glove as a target for the pitcher.
3. Fields ball that is hit close to home plate. Many times the catcher will be the one to field a bunted ball.
4. When there is not a baserunner on first base the catcher backs up the first baseman. This means that when the ball is hit the catcher runs down behind first base in case the first baseman misses the ball when it is thrown.

Pitcher

1. Becomes a fielder when the ball is hit close to him.
2. When the first baseman is off base fielding a ball, the pitcher covers first base.
3. When there is a runner on first base the pitcher backs up the third baseman.
4. When there is a runner on second base the pitcher backs up the catcher.
5. Covers home plate when for some reason the catcher is drawn out of position.

First Baseman

1. Plays several feet off first base when there is no baserunner on the base and plays close to the base when there is a baserunner on first base.
2. Fields balls that are hit or thrown around the area of first base.
3. When there is not a runner on first base, the first baseman backs up the second baseman when throws come in from left field and center field.

Second Baseman

1. Plays between first and second base and stands several feet back of the base line and about the same distance from second base.
2. Fields balls that are hit on the left side of second base.
3. When the ball is hit to the right side of second base, covers the base to receive the ball fielded by another player.
4. Covers second base when the ball is thrown by the catcher.
5. Goes out to receive the ball from the center fielder or the right fielder and throws it to the infield.

Shortstop

1. Plays about halfway between second base and third base and stands several feet back of the base line.
2. Fields the balls that go between second base and third base.
3. When the ball is hit on the first base side, covers second base.
4. On balls thrown from the catcher, backs up second baseman.
5. Goes out to receive the ball from the left fielder and throws it into the infield.

Third Baseman

1. Plays several feet off the base and stands about three or four feet back of the baseline.
2. Fields balls hit on left side of the field and has to work closely with the second baseman in fielding balls.
3. On high fly balls around home plate, may need to come in close to the catcher. If the catcher misses the ball the third baseman can sometimes recover it before it hits the ground.

Left Fielder

1. When balls are hit to the center field, the left fielder backs up the center fielder.
2. When it is necessary, the left fielder backs up the third baseman.

Center Fielder

1. Backs up right fielder when ball is hit to right field.
2. Backs up left fielder when ball is hit to left field.
3. When a ground ball is hit to the shortstop or second baseman the center fielder backs them up.
4. Backs up the second baseman on just about all balls that come that way.

Right Fielder

1. Is the backup for the center fielder, second baseman, and first baseman.
2. Backs up a play made at first base or second base.

TEAM PLAY

Offensive and defensive team play in baseball are somewhat different than in most other games. This is certainly true of offensive team play. While there is some chance for a batter and baserunner to work together, there are not a lot of ways where this can happen. So when we talk about offensive team play in baseball we are really concerned about individual play. The following are some of the things to think about in offensive play.

1. The player should be sure to "run out" all hits. It may look like an easy out, but it is just possible that the first baseman will drop the ball.
2. The player should run as fast as possible and run over first base on a short hit.

3. The baserunner should be sure to know how many outs have been made when on base.
4. A hitter should try to be a place hitter, and try to hit the ball where the fielders are not playing.

The following are some things to remember about defensive play.

1. A player should know whom to back up when a play is made.
2. A player needs to think ahead about what to do. This means that a player needs to know the number of outs and players on base.
3. A play should be made on a player who is closest to a score; that is, if a player is running for home a play should be made on that player.
4. The ball should be thrown to the base where the baserunner is going.
5. The players should talk to each other on the field so that each is sure what to do.

SOFTBALL

Softball is a form of baseball, but it is different in the following ways.

1. A ball larger and softer is used rather than the hard baseball.
2. The distance between the bases in softball is 55 feet, while in baseball this distance is 90 feet.
3. The pitching distance is 43 feet for men and 35 feet for women. The pitching distance for baseball is 60½ feet.
4. Pitching in softball is done with the underarm throwing pattern. The overarm throwing pattern is allowed in all other parts of the game.

Softball was started in the early 1900s by American professional baseball players. They played softball to keep in practice during the off-season. At that time the game was called *Indoor Baseball*. It was a good game because it gave professional players a chance to practice during the winter months.

During the late 1920s the game became very popular in Canada. Players from that country began to play the game outdoors on playgrounds and it became known as *Playground ball*. Sometime later the name of the game was changed to *Softball* and that is the name it goes by today.

The size of the softball can be from 12 inches to 32 inches in circumference. For young players the distance of the baseline is arbitrary. Ordinarily, the larger the ball the shorter the baselines are likely to be.

The skills for softball are essentially the same as they are for baseball. As mentioned previously, the one main exception is pitching. Pitching is done with the underarm throwing pattern, which was explained in Chapter 3. At the start of the pitch the feet should be parallel. For a right-handed pitcher the right arm is swung back. The body turns slightly. The right arm is brought forward, and the ball is released off the ends of the fingers. The ball should be at about the level of the hip when it is pitched. The right foot is brought up so that the pitcher is in a good position to field the ball if it is hit by the batter.

GAMES TO PRACTICE BASEBALL SKILLS

Any of the old neighborhood games are baseball-type games. Many children have probably played some of them at one time or another. The following games have been found useful for practicing several of the skills required in baseball.

Bases on Balls

This game is played on a softball diamond. There are two teams of any number on each team. One team is in the field while the other is at bat. A tennis ball or rubber playground ball can be used. The batter throws the ball up as in fungo batting and hits it with the hand into the field. The player in the field who receives the ball runs and places the ball on home plate. The batter runs the bases after hitting the ball. The batter gets a point for every base touched before the fielder places the ball on home plate. There are no outs in this game, and every player has a chance to bat. When all players on each team have had a chance to bat, the teams change places. As many innings as desired can be played.

Hit Pin Baseball

This game is like softball except that objects such as ten pins or empty milk cartons are used rather than bases. The pitcher throws the ball in easily so that the batter can hit it. After hitting the ball the batter starts around the bases. The fielder who receives the ball throws it to first base. The first baseman knocks the object over with the ball and throws the ball to second base. The game goes on until the ball has gone around all the bases and the objects have been knocked down. The batter stops when the object (base) he or she is headed for is knocked down. There are no outs, and every member of the team gets to bat in each inning.

Base Run

There are four players on a team in this game. These players are a catcher, first baseman, second baseman, and third baseman. The catcher stands on home base, and the basemen are on their bases. There is a runner who tries to get around the bases once while the ball goes around twice. The runner starts when the catcher throws the ball to first. The first baseman throws the ball to second, and so on. The baserunner tries to beat the ball. If the runner gets around once before the ball gets around twice he or she scores one point for the team. After the four runners have had a chance to run, they become basemen.

Beatball Baseball

This game can have seven or more players on each team. If the batter hits the pitch he or she runs to first, second, third and home without stopping. The fielders get the ball to the first baseman, who must touch the base with the ball in his or her hands. The first baseman throws the ball to the second baseman on base. The second baseman throws to third base. The third baseman throws to the catcher. If the ball gets home before the runner, then the runner is out. The ball must beat the runner home and not just the bases ahead of the runner. If the runner beats the ball home he or she scores a run for the team. All of the other rules of baseball apply.

Flies and Grounders

Any number of players can play this game. There is one batter, and the other players go into the field. The batter fungo bats the ball into the field. The player closest to the ball calls out, "Mine!" If the ball is caught on the fly, it counts five points. If it is caught on first bounce from a fly, it counts three points. If a grounder is caught, it counts one point. When a player gets 15 points, he or she becomes the batter.

The standard game of baseball played with more or less the same rules from youth baseball through high school, college and professional leagues has for decades been a widely popular sport in the United States and now also in other nations. Its popularity in the US is seen in its nickname, which for some decades has been "America's Pastime" game.

ENDNOTES

1. *The Columbia Encyclopedia*, Columbia University Press, sixth edition, 2000, p. 248, Ed. Paul Lagasse.
2. First Pitch Is Now Scheduled For 1823, *The Washington Post*, July 9, 2001, p. D2.
3. Rowen, Fred, If the Glove Fits, *KidsPost*, May 4, 2001, p. C13.

Chapter 6

BASKETBALL

It is very interesting how some games got their start and also how they got their name. Many games that we play in the United States began in other countries. Basketball is one of the few games that got its start in America.

The game of basketball was invented by Dr. James Naismith in Springfield, Massachusetts in 1891. When Dr. Naismith was a student, the teacher of one of his classes had suggested an assignment that called for the invention of a game that could be played indoors with a small number of players. Dr. Naismith designed the game of basketball for that class assignment. It was invented as a game that could be used to fill in the time between the end of football season in the fall and the start of baseball in the spring.

In the beginning, the game of basketball was much different than it is today. There were nine players on each team. They were allowed to throw, bat, or pass the ball. The first game was played with peach baskets, and this is how it got the name of basketball. After a time, the rules changed so that there were five on a men's team and six on a women's team. In modern times there are also five on women's teams. In the early days the number of players sometimes depended on how much space there was for playing.

When women played the game with six players on a team, three players were on the *defensive* end of the court and three were on the *offensive* end. At the time it was said that females did not have the stamina to play the full length of the court. Eventually, this notion was dispelled and the women's game became the same as that of the men.

Originally, the game was played only by grown men and women. Today it is played by children as well as adults, although the rules may be modified for young players.

Interest in the game of basketball has spread so widely that it is now played in many countries around the world. In fact, it has become a very important part of the Olympic Games. People of all ages and in many nations enjoy trying to put a ball through a basket.

Basketball as played today can take place on a court as small as 42 feet by 72 feet. The largest size is 50 feet by 90 feet. The basketball goals at either end of the court are 10 feet high with each team having its own goal. It is interesting to note that this is one dimension of the game that has never changed; that is, when the game began the goal was 10 feet and this height still remains the same today. Sometimes for young players the goals may be eight or nine feet. This lower height can make it easier for them to get the ball into the basket. The regular size of the ball is 29½ inches in circumference. Smaller balls are sometimes used for young players and are also used in women's basketball. In this general regard, Benham[1] reviewed the literature regarding the effect that scaling down equipment has on a child's basketball performance. It was concluded that (1) a decrease in the basketball size and weight appears to benefit young children with less absolute body size and strength by requiring less force to be applied when shooting or passing and improved ball control skills, and (2) a decrease in the goal height appears to benefit children's shooting accuracy.

The popularity of basketball among children apparently is surpassed by no other sport. For example, recently when 7,500 children were asked in a *Sports Illustrated For Kids* poll to name their favorite athlete and the athlete they would like to be for a day, their top three choices were professional basketball players Michael Jordan, Magic Johnson, and Scottie Pippen. This is also borne out in our own studies which consistently show that basketball is by far the most popular sport among 9 to 12 year olds.

BASKETBALL SKILLS

The game of basketball requires many different kinds of skills. These skills include passing, catching, shooting, dribbling, pivoting, and guarding.

Passing

Passing simply means that the ball is transferred from one player to another. There are many different kinds of passes and each one has its own purpose. The kind of pass used will depend upon two things. The first thing is the distance the ball has to travel. Second the position in which the ball is caught may cause the player to choose the kind of pass to make. The following are some of the more widely used passes.

Chest Pass

This pass is probably the one most often used in basketball. It is good to use when the ball is to be passed a short distance. The ball is held chest high. The fingers grip the ball and are spread lightly over the center of the ball. The thumbs are close together. The elbows are bent and close to the body. In the passing action the arms go forward from the shoulders and the elbows straighten. The ball is released with a snap of the wrists. The ball can be passed a greater distance if the knees are bent and a short step is taken with one foot.

Bounce Pass

This pass can be done with one or both hands. It is probably better to use both hands as this makes it less difficult to control the ball. In this pass a bounce is used so that the ball can bounce into another player's hands. When two hand are used, it is done about the same way as the chest pass. The difference is that the ball is passed low to hit the floor rather than chest high. This is not an easy pass to make, and it takes lots of practice. The passer must judge the place on the floor to bounce the ball. It is a good idea to make the ball hit the floor about three-fourths of the distance from the passer to the catcher. This kind of pass will cause the ball to be caught at about the waist. Some beginners make the mistake of bouncing the ball straight downward rather than pushing it forward. The good feature about the bounce pass is that is sometimes allows the passer to get the ball to the catcher before it can be blocked.

One-Handed Underarm Pass

This pass is done with the underarm throwing pattern explained in Chapter 3. Because the ball is too large to be gripped, the other hand is placed on top of the ball. This will keep it from falling out of the throwing hand. The other hand is taken away when the ball is brought forward. This pass is good for short distances to get the ball quickly to another player.

Shoulder Pass

This pass is sometimes called the baseball pass or the one-hand overarm pass. It is done with the overarm throwing pattern explained in Chapter 3. This pass is not used too often by young players because it is hard to control. It is useful when passing a distance. If a teammate breaks away and gets down the floor it can be a good pass to get the ball there more quickly. It should be remembered that as a general rule shorter passes are better than long passes. It should also be remembered that the longer the pass the greater chance it has to be caught by a member of the other team.

The shoulder pass is begun with one foot just ahead of the other. The hand that is not used to throw the ball is used to steady it. This helps the passer to keep from losing control of the ball. The ball is brought forward above the shoulder and past the ear. When the ball is released there should be a snap of the wrist the same as in the chest pass.

Two-Handed Overhead Pass

In this pass the ball is held approximately over the head with both hands. The fingers are spread above the center of the ball, and the elbows are slightly bent. The passer steps forward with one foot if there is space to do so and passes the ball forward at the same time. At the end of the pass the arms and fingers will be pointing upward. This is a good pass to use when the distance is longer than is needed for the chest pass.

Catching

The reader might wish to review the general discussion about catching in Chapter 3. Some of those procedures will be repeated because of the way they apply to basketball. An important factor in catching in the game of basketball is that the catcher should move to meet the ball. This movement is sometimes called *cutting* or *going to meet the ball* and will shorten the distance the ball has to travel. Also, it will help to shut off a player of the other team who tries to block or intercept the ball. When the ball is caught it should be brought in close to the body. This will help to keep the person who is guarding the passer from getting the ball.

It has already been mentioned how the hands should be held when a ball is caught at the waist, or below the waist. Usually a basketball is caught in the last two positions, above or below the waist. When catching a basketball above the waist the hands are forward toward the ball with fingers pointing up. The knees are slightly bent; the feet are apart; and the body leans slightly forward. When the ball is caught the fingers are spread, and the hands and arms give with the ball. This helps to slow the force of the ball and make it less difficult to control.

In catching the basketball below the waist, the fingers point downward and are well spread and the hands and the arms give with the ball when it is caught. The player should try not to shift the hands on the ball because he or she might want to pass it quickly with the same motion.

Shooting

Because putting the ball through the hoop is the method of scoring, shooting is obviously one of the most important skills.

The basic patterns of basket shooting are those of throwing which were discussed in Chapter 3. Three things need to be remembered. First, allowance must be made for the angle when the ball is released. The second thing is how much force is needed to send the ball to the basket. The third important thing to remember is that the eyes should be kept on the rim of the goal.

There are about five different kinds of shots in the game of basketball that will be discussed here.

1. Two-handed underhand shot.
2. Two-handed chest shot.
3. One-handed push shot.

4. Lay-up shot.
5. Jump shot.

Two-Handed Underhand Shot

This is probably the easiest way for young players to shoot. It could be useful as a free throw shot. It is seldom used in today's game of basketball when the ball is in play because it is easy to block. The ball is held about waist high. The fingers of both hands are under the ball with the thumbs pointing upward. The knees are bent and the ball is brought downward between the legs. The ball is then brought upward, and the knees become straight. The ball is released when the arms are straight toward the basket.

Even though it is a good way to shoot free throws, most players of high school age and older use other kinds of shots for free throws. One big exception was Rick Barry, the former basketball star of the Houston Rockets. He used the two-handed underhand shot for free throws, and the fact that he was one of the best "foul shooters" in all of basketball is reason enough for believing that it was for some players a good way to shoot free throws.

Two-Handed Chest Shot

This shot is a good one for beginners because the ball is easy to control. The two-handed chest shot is like the chest pass, but the angle where the ball is released is different. The ball is held in both hands about chest high. The ball is tipped back on the fingers, which are spread and above the center of the ball. The ball is then pushed toward the goal. The shooter tries to get a proper arch on the flight of the ball. Either foot can be ahead of the other, or the feet can be together. The knees should be bent. When the ball is released the legs are straightened. At the end of the shot, the arms are stretched, and the fingers point upward toward the basket.

One-Handed Push Shot

The ball is balanced by the fingers of the shooting hand. The other hand supports the ball from underneath. One foot is slightly ahead of the other. The knees are bent slightly and the feet are spread at a distance where the shooter feels comfortable. Most of the weight is on the front foot. The hand underneath the ball is taken away as the ball is pushed toward the basket. When the ball is released, the fingers of the shooting hand point toward the basket. The arm is stretched to full length upward. This shot may not be easy because it is harder to control the ball with one hand than it is with two. However, if the shooter can control the ball, this shot is difficult to guard against, the reason being that the shot starts high and the shooter can release the ball quickly.

Lay-Up Shot

This shot is a little bit like the one-handed push shot. The ball is aimed at the backboard when the shooter is close in under the basket. The reason for this aim is that the ball is banked against the backboard into the basket; that is, the shooter "lays" the ball on the backboard. The right-handed shooter takes off close to the basket from the left foot and jumps toward the goal. For the left-handed shooter the takeoff is from the right foot. The player usually comes to the basket from the side with a bounce of the ball, or he or she may catch a pass from a teammate running in. It is probably a good idea to practice the shot first without the jump. This will give the shooter an idea of where the ball should hit the backboard so that it will drop into the basket.

Jump Shot

The jump shot uses the same movement as the one-handed push shot. The shot is made after jumping into the air from the floor with both feet. The jump shot is difficult to guard against because the ball is higher when the shooter releases it. At the same time it is a more difficult shot to make and takes a great deal of practice. It is probably the most frequently used shot from out on the court by players of high school age and older.

Dribbling

Dribbling means that a player controls the ball by bouncing it, usually several times. The fingers are well spread so that it will be easier to control the ball. The knees are bent to keep the body low. The body leans forward;

the ball is held just a little higher than the knees. The beginning dribbler will probably need to keep his or her eyes on the ball. After the skill is learned, the player should practice keeping the head up. The first bounce is started by laying the ball well out in front and pushing with the dribbling hand. The ball is *pushed* forward to the floor and not *slapped* downward. If the defender is close to the dribbler, then the dribbling will need to be initiated and maintained with the dribbler's body positioned between the ball and the defender in order to shield the ball from the more aggressive defender.

Pivoting

The basic skill of pivoting was described in Chapter 3. In basketball, pivoting is used to change direction when a player is standing in place. It takes place when a player who is holding the ball steps once, or more, in any direction with the same foot. The other foot is the pivot foot and stays in contact with the floor. The weight of the body is equally placed on both feet. The ball is held firmly with the fingers of both hands. The elbows point outward to help protect the ball from a player on the other team. The player can turn in any direction on the pivot foot. He or she should not drag the pivot foot because this movement is the same as walking with the ball (traveling).

Guarding

Up to this point the discussion has been about skills with the ball. The skill of guarding is used to try to keep an opponent from shooting, passing, or dribbling. An important rule in guarding is this: *the player should try to keep between the basket and the player being guarded.* In guarding, the feet are spread, and the knees are bent. The arms are outstretched to the sides. One arm can be up and the other down. In this position the player is ready to move in any direction. That movement is usually done with the skill of sliding, which was described in Chapter 3. When the person a player is guarding gets the ball the player should try to get about two to three feet away. In the guarding position the player is ready not only to block a pass or shot, but also to stop a dribble. In the case of a "pressing" or tight defense, the defender might place himself or herself with very little space between the defender and the person with the ball and/or the offensive person to whom the pass is to be made.

Rebounding

When a shot does not go into the basket it will probably rebound back to the playing area. Rebounding is a skill used to try to get the ball after it has bounced off the backboard of the basket. This is one of the most difficult skills to learn. The reason for this is that the player must time the jump and rebound of the ball. A player who is able to time these two movements well will be in the right spot to get the ball. The player jumps from the floor and stretches the arms toward the basket. After the ball is caught it should be brought in close to the body. When the player has the ball and the feet are on the floor, he or she should usually bend forward to protect the ball. If a player is successful in rebounding at his or her basket the team will control the ball – an offensive rebound. Getting a rebound at the other team's basket means that a player will have taken the ball so that the other team cannot shoot again right away – a defensive rebound. Although it helps to be tall in rebounding, being able to jump high and time the jump are also very important.

TEAM PLAY

Obviously, team play is very important in basketball. This means both offensive and defensive team play. The following are some important things to remember about *offensive* team play.

1. Players should try to be aware at all times where their teammates are on the floor.
2. Players should be thinking about getting into an empty space to get away from the person guarding them.
3. When a player passes the ball he or she should keep moving and not stand around.

4. Players will usually have more success with short passes than with long ones.

5. When shooting, the player should make sure that he or she has a good chance of making the basket. Otherwise, there should be a pass to another player.

6. When a player has the ball there are only three things to do: pass, shoot, or dribble. The player must decide quickly what is the best thing to do. If there is not a good shot it is a good idea to pass the ball. Dribbling is often used when, for some reason, the player is not able to pass the ball and does not have a desirable shot. The exception, of course, is when a player dribbles the ball up the court to start offensive play.

The following are some important things to remember about *defensive* play.

1. Most guarding is done on the other team's offensive area of the floor. Usually there is not a need to guard all over the floor. There are certain times to use a pressing defense (guarding all over the floor or full court press). Sometimes a team will do this near the end of the game or to upset the opposing team's offense and to attempt to more quickly regain possession of the ball.

2. A player should always know which opposing player he or she is supposed to guard.

3. When guarding, a player should never cross the feet. The skill of sliding should be used instead.

4. Sometimes it is a good idea to have one person back in order to guard against a "fast break" (or fast movement of the ball back down court) when the other team regains possession of the ball.

5. In guarding, the player should always try to keep between the basket and the player being guarded.

GAMES TO PRACTICE BASKETBALL SKILLS

Most of the basketball skills that have been discussed can be practiced by one person alone. However, with some of the skills it is better to have a partner. If there are several people, they can execute more complex drills or play games to practice the skills.

The games that are explained here are just a few examples of many possibilities. Many times players can make up games of their own that are good for practicing certain basketball skills. The following games use one or more of the skills of passing, catching, dribbling, shooting, and guarding. They do not need to be played on a regular basketball court.

Bear in the Circle

Two circles are formed with each circle as a team with four or more players. One member of the other team, the bear, stands in the center of each circle. The players in the circle pass the ball to each other and the bear tries to touch it. If the bear touches the ball, a point is scored for that team. To begin with, players decide how long they will play the game. At the end of that time the team with the highest score is the winner. Everyone on both teams should have a turn at being the bear.

Keep Away

There can be as many teams as desired in this game with four or more players on a team. It is better to have more teams so that there are not many players on a team. This way more players will get a chance to handle the ball. Play starts with one of the teams having the ball. This team passes the ball around to its own players. Players of all the other teams try to get the ball. If a member of one of the teams gets the ball, that team starts play again with the ball. All of the rules of basketball are used, and the idea of the game is to see which team can keep the ball for the longest amount of time.

Tag Ball

This game is like *Keep Away* except that one member on each of the teams is picked to be *It*. The purpose of the game is to tag the person on a team who is *It* with the ball. When this happens the tagging team scores a point. All of the rules of basketball are used. The ball can be advanced to *It* by passing or dribbling. All of the players who are *It* should stand out in some way, perhaps with an armband, so that the others can tell easily which player is *It*.

Half-Court Basketball

All of the rules of basketball are used. The only difference from the regular game is that only one-half of the court is used. Both teams use the same goal. When a goal is made or the other team gets the ball, the other team must start again with the ball. Play usually begins again somewhere around the free throw line or at the top of the circle. This is a good game if one has a basketball goal in the yard, in the driveway, or if one end of the basketball court is not available for play.

The game of basketball, a truly American sport now played around the world, is a widely popular sport for participants at many age levels and for spectators of all ages. It is a good youth sport to teach teamwork and develop physical conditioning for young players.

ENDNOTE

1. Benham, Tami, Modification of Basketball Equipment and Childhood Performance, *Proceedings of the National Alliance for Health, Physical Education, Recreation, and Dance*, Cincinnati, Ohio, April 1986.

Chapter 7

SOCCER

The game of soccer is different than most games in that it is played mainly with the feet, while most other games are played by using the hands to control the ball. In soccer, the arms are free to enhance balance.

Two prominent child developmental specialists, Dawne Larkin and Debbi Hoare[1] maintain that this is a very good activity for children who have fine motor control problems with the upper limbs and hands. They believe that the game of soccer allows children with this type of movement challenge (dysfunction) to work within the range of their abilities and circumvent their disabilities. It is also interesting to note that there has been some experimentation with blind children in the game of soccer. A "beeper" is attached to the ball so that visually impaired children can follow the movement of the ball by the sound.

When the game of soccer first started it was called *Association Football*. The rules for this game were made in the year 1863 by the *London Football Association*. Later, the word "Association: was shortened to "Assoc," which was later changed to soccer."

Soccer is very popular and is played all over the world. It probably has its greatest popularity in certain South American countries and in some European countries. In more recent years it has become very popular in the United States. This popularity is particularly true of the game as played by children. In fact, our studies show that it is the fourth most popular sport among 10-year-old boys and girls. This can be attributed in part to the holding of the Soccer World Cup championships in the United States in the summer of 1995 and other major soccer events on television in recent years – as well as the emergence of men's and women's professional soccer teams across America. In this regard, it is interesting to note that a national poll showed that 44 percent of Americans watched at least one World Cup game on television; and 53 percent became more interested in soccer than before the World Cup was played in the United States. Add to this the fact that the United States Women's team won the world championship in 1999, and there is no wonder about the rise in the popularity of soccer.

Soccer is played on a field 130 yards by 100 yards. This is the largest the field can be. The smallest the field is supposed to be is 100 yards by 50 yards. There is a goal at each end of the field. These goals are made up of two posts, which are 8 yards apart with a crossbar on the posts, which is 8 feet above the ground. A net is attached to this goal to stop the ball after it has entered the goal and also to more easily recognize that the ball has entered the goal. The game is played with a round ball, which is about 27 to 28 inches in circumference.

To score a goal a player must get the ball through the goal and under the crossbar. This must be done with the feet or head. There are 11 players on each team and they move the ball by kicking it with their feet or hitting it with their head. There is very little use of the hands. However, the hands can be used by the goalkeeper (goalie). Also when the ball goes out-of-bounds it can be thrown in with the hands.

The game is often modified for young players. Many times a smaller playing area is used, and a lighter ball can be used. Sometimes the rules allow for more use of the hands.

OFFENSIVE SOCCER SKILLS

There are three ways that the ball can be moved. These are (1) kicking, (2) with the head which is called "heading," and (3) with the hands to "throw in" from out-or-bounds.

Kicking

There are about six different kinds of kicks that are used in soccer: (1) kicking with the instep, (2) kicking with the inside of the foot, (3) kicking with the outside of the foot, (4) punting, (5) volley kick, and (6) foot dribbling.

Kicking with the Instep
Kicking with the instep of the foot is probably the kick that is most used in soccer. It can be used for passing the ball to a teammate and for shooting at the goal. The foot *not* used for kicking is even with the ball. The kicking leg is back, and the body leans forward. The ankle is downward so that the instep meets the ball.

Kicking with the Inside of the Foot
The inside edge of the foot meets the ball with the toes of the kicking foot turned out. The leg is bent slightly at the knee. When the inside of the foot meets the ball, the leg swings across in front of the body. Just as the foot meets the ball in front of the body, the knee is straightened. The foot should meet the ball just below the center. Usually the kicker takes a short run up to the ball while it is on the ground and not moving. In kicking the ball with the inside of the foot, the ball can be kicked a long way. This kind of kick can also be used to make a short pass to a teammate or to try to kick for a goal.

Kicking with the Outside of the Foot
This kick is used mainly for short distances to get the ball to a teammate. It can also be used to get the ball away from an opponent who is running toward the player. The foot that is *not* being used to kick is about 6 or 8 inches behind the ball and to the side of it. The knee of the kicking leg is bent. The kicking leg swings across in front of the other leg. The outside of the foot meets the ball as the kicking foot swings passed the other leg.

Punting

This is the kick that we called "kick from hands" in Chapter 3. The goalkeeper is the only player allowed to punt the ball. The punt is used to clear the ball over the heads of other players down the field.

Punting is somewhat like kicking with the instep. The difference is that the ball is held out in front and dropped as it is kicked. If the goalkeeper punts with the right foot, the ball is held out in front of the right leg, a little above the waist. A step is taken on the left foot and the right leg is brought back. When the ball is dropped the punter swings the right leg forward and upward. The foot hits the ball with the instep of the foot.

Volley Kick

The volley is a kick that is made while the ball is in the air. Because it is very hard to kick the ball while it is in the air, sometimes the volley kick is not always allowed in soccer games with younger players. When it is used, the following is one way to do it: He or she faces the ball as it comes in and leans forward slightly. When the ball gets to the player, the leg of the kicking foot is raised, and the weight is shifted to the other foot. The knee is bent slightly and the toes point downward. The foot meets the ball at the top of the instep, and the foot goes forward and upward.

Dribbling

Dribbling is a way to control the ball with the feet when moving along. It is a very light kick. The foot just touches the ball and moves it along.

To begin the dribble, the weight of the body is equal on both feet. The ball should be kept about one foot in front of the dribbler. The arms can be out to the side to help keep one's balance. The head should be over the ball. The ball is tapped easily with either foot. The player dribbles first with one foot and then the other. He or she can use the inside or outside of the foot, but it is usually easier to dribble with the inside of the foot.

Heading

Heading the soccer ball means that it is hit with the front or side of the forehead. Sometimes heading is not allowed in soccer games played by younger players. The main reason for this is that sometimes young players do not do it well, predisposing themselves to injury. If it is used in soccer for younger players, perhaps it should be done with a ball that is much lighter and softer than a regular soccer ball, or with a helmet for protection.

As the ball comes toward the player, the head is dropped back. The arms are raised. The weight is shifted to the back foot. The next move is to bring the body forward and upward. At this time the head meets the ball. The ball is met with the side or front of the forehead. At the end of the movement the player lands on both feet and the ankles and knees are bent and the arms are out to the sides for balance.

The Throw In

When the ball goes out-of-bounds over the sidelines it has to be put in play again. It is put in play with the *throw in* as the player stands out-of-bounds. The throw in should be done from behind the head with both hands. Part of both feet must be on the ground until the player lets the ball go.

The throw in for soccer is very much like the two-handed overhead pass in basketball, as described in Chapter 6. The throw in is started with one foot ahead of the other. The ball is held above the head with both hands. As the ball is thrown in the player shifts the weight to the front leg. A snap of the wrists will get more force behind the ball.

DEFENSIVE SOCCER SKILLS

The way to stop the ball in soccer is called *trapping*. There are many kinds of traps, including (1) body traps, (2) foot traps, and (3) leg traps.

Body Traps

Body traps are a way to stop the ball with the body. It is done in a way so that the ball will drop to the ground at a place where the player can quickly dribble or kick it. The body trap is used when the ball is coming from a high volley, or when a player does not want a high ball to get past him or her.

The body is straight, the weight is on both feet and the eyes are kept on the ball. As the ball comes in waist high or above, the body is moved backward. The weight is not on the heels, and the arms can be out to the side for balance. Just as the ball meets the body, the player should "give" with it. At the same time the player takes a short jump backward. The player tries to make a "pocket" for the ball as it hits the chest. When girls use the body trap it is a good idea for them to fold their arms over their chest. This way the ball hits their folded arms. If the body trap is done in the right way the ball will more or less roll down the front of the player. He or she should then be ready to dribble or kick.

Foot Traps

Foot traps are used to stop a ball that is rolling or bouncing along the ground. The two ways to trap the ball with the feet are (1) with the sole of the foot, and (2) with the side of the foot.

Trapping with the Sole of the Foot

The player first needs to line up with the ball so that it is coming straight in. When the ball reaches the player, he or she raises the foot that will be used to trap the ball. This foot is about 8 inches from the ground with the toes pointing upward. The player quickly brings the sole of the foot down on the ball. The ball is trapped between the ground and the sole of the foot. It is best to use this trap when the ball is moving slowly.

Trapping with the Side of the Foot

This trap is pretty much done the same way as the trap with the sole of the foot. The main difference is in the way the ball comes to the player. It is better to use the side of the foot if the ball is bouncing from the side. Also, it might be better to use this trap when the ball is coming in fairly fast. The weight is on the foot that in *not* going to trap the ball. The player turns the foot that is to trap the ball outward so that the ball meets the inside of the foot. As soon as the ball touches the foot the player should allow the foot to "give" with the ball. With practice one should be able to make the ball stop where he or she wants it to stop. If the ball bounces off the foot it means that the player did not allow the foot to "give" with the ball.

Leg Traps

There are two ways of trapping the ball with the legs: (1) with one leg (or the single leg trap), and (2) with both legs (or the double leg trap).

Single Leg Trap

In the single leg trap, the player tries to get in line with the ball. The foot of the trapping leg is placed slightly back of the other foot. Just the toes of this foot touch the ground. The knees of both legs are bent. If trapping with the right leg, the player should turn slightly to the left. When the ball meets the leg, the lower part of the leg, or shin, presses against the ball and traps it. If done correctly, the ball should be placed in front of the player where he or she can kick it or dribble it.

Double Leg Trap

When using the double leg trap the feet should be slightly apart with the toes pointing outward. The knees are bent slightly more than in the single leg trap. The reason for this position is to trap the ball against the ground with both shins. After the trap the body is raised up straight. The ball will be right in front where the player can dribble or kick it. It is a good idea to put the arms out to the side.. This will help balance the player and keep him or her from tilting awkwardly or falling.

Tackling

In soccer, tackling means that the player tries to take the ball way from an opponent. It is called tackling the ball. When a player is good at tackling he or she can cause another player to make a poor kick, to overrun the ball, or to otherwise lose control of the ball. That is the purpose of tackling the ball. The two ways of tackling the ball are: (1) the straight tackle and (2) the hook tackle.

Straight Tackle

In the straight tackle the player tries to get in front of an opponent who is dribbling. He or she tries to put a foot on the ball. This movement is somewhat like trapping the ball with the sole of the foot. If one can get a foot on the ball he or she should try to kick it or hold it until the dribbler overruns the ball.

Hook Tackle

In the hook tackle the player also tries to get in front of the opponent who is dribbling. A quick step is taken to one side. There is a reach in with one leg and that leg is used as a "hook." The player tries to draw the ball out to the side. The other leg must be bent so as to reach in a great distance with the hooking leg.

TEAM PLAY

Just as in the game of basketball, team play is very important in the game of soccer. This means *offensive* team play when one team has the ball and *defensive* team play when the other team has the ball. The following are some important things to remember about offensive team play.

1. When possible try to use short kicks. It is easier for the other team to get the ball when a long kick is used.
2. Try to make sure that the ball is under control before trying to kick it.
3. When kicking it to a teammate, try to kick the ball ahead of him or her. This allows the player to take the pass "on the move."
4. The player should know where his or her place is on the field and try to move effectively within the area.

The following are some important things to remember in defensive play.

1. Get ready to tackle the ball as soon as a member of the other team gets it.
2. Always be thinking about the kind of trap to use on the ball and be prepared to use it.
3. When getting control of the ball from a member of the other team, get it to a teammate as soon as possible.

GAMES TO PRACTICE SOCCER SKILLS

Many of the soccer skills can be practiced by one person. In some of them it is probably better to have a partner. There are many games children can play to help them with soccer skills.

Line Soccer

In this game the players will be able to practice kicking, dribbling, and trapping. There are two teams with about eight players on a team. The playing area should be about 30 feet to 60 feet. The two teams form lines facing each other. The idea of the game is for a player to kick the ball over the other team's goal line.

To start the game, the ball is placed in the center of the playing field. Two players go to the center of the field and put their right foot on the ball. A signal is given, and each of these players tries to kick the ball across the other team's goal line. These two players can run all over the field kicking or dribbling the ball. All the other players try to keep the ball from going over the goal line. They do this by trapping or kicking the ball. Two points are scored when a player kicks the ball over the other goal line. Only the players in the center are allowed to score. The players should try to keep the ball below the waist of the other players. It is a foul if the ball is touched with the hands or arms. Kicking the ball over the head is also a foul. The penalty for a foul is a free kick, which is made from the center of the field. The game is over when everyone has had a chance to be one of the two players in the center of the field.

Corner Kickball

Corner Kickball is a good game to practice the skills of dribbling and kicking. There are two teams of about 10 players on each team. The playing area can be about 40 feet by 75 feet. The idea of the game is to kick the ball through the other team's end zone. The size of the end zone is about 15 feet from the front line to the back line.

To begin the game the ball is placed in the center of the field. On a signal, a corner player from each team runs to the center and tries to kick or dribble the ball into the other's end zone. The other players stay in the end zone and try to stop the ball with any part of the body other than the hands and arms. When a goal is scored, two other players come to the center. If a goal is not scored after a certain amount of time, two new players come to the center of the field to play the ball. It is a foul if there is tripping, pushing or touching the ball with the hands. If there is a foul, the other team gets a free kick from 15 yards out.

Circle Trap

Any number of players can be used in this game. All of the players but one form a circle. This one player stands in the center of the circle. One of the players making the circle starts the game by rolling the ball across the circle. The players making the circle try to keep the ball moving by kicking it to one another. The player in the center of the circle tries to trap the ball. If able to do so, he or she changes places with the player who was the last one to kick the ball. If the ball goes out of the circle the one nearest it goes to the center of the circle. If the player in the center of the circle is not able to trap the ball after a period of time, another player should be chosen to go to the center.

Circle Soccer

A circle is formed with any number of players. The players kick a ball around in the circle as quickly as they can. The idea of the game is to keep the ball from going out of the circle. If the ball goes out of the circle it counts a point against the two players on either side of the ball where it went out of the circle. This means that when the ball goes out of the circle between two players each one gets a point scored against him or her. The ball should be kept on the ground when kicking it. It should not be kicked above the waist. The game can be made more interesting by using two balls at the same time.

Hit Pin Soccer

Any number of players can be used in this game. The number of players is divided into four teams. Each team stands in line side by side. All four teams make a square. The players face inward. All of the players of each team have a number; that is, if there are six players on a team one player is number one, another is number two and so on. A leader is chosen, and he or she drops the ball in the center of the square. At the same time the leader calls a number. All four of the players with this number run to the center and try to get the ball through any side of the square. The players at the side of the square are goalkeepers. They can use their hands to stop the ball. As soon as a score is made by getting the ball through any side of the square, another number is called. The member of the team who got the ball through the side of the square scores a point for his or her team. The game is played for a certain amount of time or until every player's number is called. Square Soccer is a good game to practice kicking, trapping, and goal tending.

Soccer continues to increase in popularity and participation throughout the United States, particularly among American youth. It is an excellent sport to develop fitness and the concept of team play and cooperation.

ENDNOTE

1. Larkin, Dawne and Hoare, Debbi, *Out of Step*, Nedlands, Western Australia, Active Life Foundation, 1991.

Chapter 8

VOLLEYBALL

Like basketball, the game of volleyball got its start in the United States. It was invented in 1895, four years after the game of basketball by William Morgan while he was teaching at the YMCA in Holyoke, Massachusetts.

The reader may recall that basketball was started as an indoor game that could be used to fill in between the end of football season in the fall and baseball season in the spring. It is believed that Mr. Morgan started the game of volleyball for those who were not interested in playing basketball.

Today, volleyball is one of the world's leading sports. One of the reasons for its popularity is that it is a game that can be played by people of all ages. Young and old alike seem to get a great deal of enjoyment out of hitting the ball back and forth across the net. While it started as an indoor game, it is now played on playgrounds, in parks, on the beach, as well as many other places. Volleyball has become so popular that millions of people of all ages all over the world play the game. It has become one of the important team sports in the Olympic Games.

The game got its name because the ball is volleyed back and forth across a net with the hands. This action is called volleying. The idea of the game is to volley the ball back and forth with each team trying to score points. Points are scored by placing the ball in such a way that the other team cannot return it before it hits the surface area.

The game is played on a court 60 feet in length by 30 feet in width. A net is placed over the middle of the court at a height of eight feet. The net can be placed an any height for young players, depending upon their age and skill. For beginners, a lightweight plastic ball or beachball can be used.

There are six players on a team. Three of these are in the front line, and three are in the back line. Players change their positions on the court at certain times during the game. This gives all players a chance to play in different positions in the front line and the back line. The ball can be hit three times by players on one team. The third person to hit it must get it over the net. One player cannot hit the ball two times in succession. It does not have to be hit three times, but it is often best to do so. The reason for this is that it makes for better team play.

In 1971 the game of mini-volleyball was developed. This game is about the same as regular volleyball except that it is played on a smaller court. The net is usually five to six feet in height. There are three or four players on a side. In many places, younger players take part in mini-volleyball before they get into the regular game of volleyball. In a number of countries the beginning age for starting to play volleyball is nine years. It has been found that mini-volleyball is best for boys and girls of this age.

VOLLEYS

There are three kinds of volleys discussed here: (1) overhead volley, (2) underhand volley and (3) forearm volley.

Overhead Volley

Some people consider the overhead volley the most important volleyball skill for young players to learn. The reason for its importance is that it is the volleying skill that is probably used the most. It is used when the ball comes in chest high or higher. It is a difficult skill and takes lots of practice.

The hands are held at about the level of the eyes. The fingers are spread with the thumbs almost touching each other. A little window is formed between the thumbs. The elbows are bent and out about the height of the shoulders. The player takes a crouch position so that the ball will come in toward the eyes. The knees are bent enough to be in a comfortable position, with one foot slightly ahead of the other. When the ball in contacted with the fingers and thumbs, the weight should be even on the balls of the feet. The player strikes the ball upward in the direction he or she is aiming. This will most likely be to a teammate if the player is the first or second person to volley the ball. The player should try to volley the ball as high as 12 to 15 feet from the floor. Some beginners make the following mistakes in the overhead volley.

1. The ball is slapped rather than pushed.
2. The ball is hit more forward than upward.
3. The body is straight when the ball is hit rather than in a crouch.
4. Using one hand instead of both.
5. The player fails to get lined up with the ball.

Underhand Volley

The underhand volley is no longer used in the game of volleyball. However, it is good to practice before trying the forearm volley. The knees are bent with the feet apart. The hands are below the waist with the palms facing upward. The fingers point downward with the little fingers together. The eyes are watching the ball. When the ball in contacted, the body weight is even on the balls of the feet. With the hands together the player tries to strike the ball upward. The arms, body and legs are extended. The movement is completed by following through with the arms and body in the direction of the ball to finish the volley.

Forearm Volley

The forearm volley is also called the *bump* or the *dig*. This volley is used mainly for four kinds of plays: (1) when the ball is low and below the waist, (2) to receive most serves, (3) to recover the ball off the net, and (4) when the player's back is toward the net.

One of the first things to consider in the forearm volley is the position of the hands. One hand is placed in the palm of the other hand. The thumbs are on top, and one thumb is placed over the other. The forearms are very close together. The body is in line with the ball, and the knees are bent. One foot can be slightly ahead of the other. The arms are lowered to prepare to receive the ball. The ball should bounce off the inside of the forearms and wrists. At the time the ball contacts the forearms it should be allowed to bounce rather than be met hard with the forearms. When contact is made with the ball, the body moves a little in the direction of the ball. It is a good idea to try to keep the ball high in the air.

SERVING

Serving is the way the ball is put into play. It means that the ball is hit with the hand by the player who is the server. The server is allowed to serve the ball from either the underhand position or the overhand position. The hand may be open or closed. Young players should begin with the underhand serve. After they have been able to serve well with the underhand serve they might want to try the overhand serve. Some younger players can do well with the overhand serve. Others may have a difficult time with it and prefer to stay with the underhand serve.

Underhand Serve

The player stands facing the net. The left foot is a little ahead of the right. If the player is left-handed, he or she should have the right foot ahead. The weight is on the rear foot. The body bends slightly forward. The ball is held in the left hand. It is in front and a little to the right of the body and the right hand should be lined up with the ball.

The serving motion is the same as the underarm throwing pattern explained in Chapter 3. The right arm swings forward and contacts the ball just below the center of it. The ball can be hit with the open hand or with the fist. If hit with the open hand, it should be with the heel of the fist. This means that the hand forms a fist with the thumb and index finger upward. To complete the serve the player follows through with the arm in the path of the ball. He or she can also step forward with the right foot after the serve.

Overhand Serve

In the overhand serve the right-handed server stands with the left foot in front. The left side is turned slightly toward the net. The ball is held in the palm of the left hand. The ball is about chest high. The weight is equal on both feet. The eyes watch the ball. The ball is tossed up two or three feet into the air above the right shoulder. When the toss is made, the weight shifts to the back foot. When the ball begins to drop, the weight is shifted to the forward foot. The arm is snapped forward, and the ball is contacted about a foot above the shoulder. The contact is made near the center of the ball with the tips of the fingers or fist. The overhead serving action is about the same as the overarm throwing pattern used in baseball or softball.

THE SET

The set means that the ball is set up for a teammate to hit it over the net. The set is usually the second hit. The ball is set up high for a teammate to spike it down over the net. In setting up the ball, the overhead volley is used. The ball should be volleyed up at a height of 12 to 15 feet. It is set up about one foot away from the net.

THE SPIKE

A spike means that the ball is hit downward as it goes into the other team's side of the court. It is a very important scoring skill, but it is quite difficult to learn. The player who is going to spike the ball stands close to the net. He or she faces the direction from where the ball is coming. When the ball starts to come down, the spiker jumps high off the floor. He or she swings the arm of the hitting hand downward, while it is still close to the net. The spiker should try to hit the ball on the top to get more force behind it. The spiker lands facing the net. He or she should be sure not to let the hand go over the net. Since this skill is very difficult to learn, it is a good idea to practice spiking the ball with the net down fairly low at first.

THE BLOCK

The block is used against a spike. The player who is going to try to block the spike faces the net. He or she tries to jump at the same time the spiker does. The player swings both arms upward with the hands close together. He or she should try to get about six inches above the net. If the blocker is successful, the ball will bounce off the hands and back into the other team's side of the court. Probably the hardest part about this skill is learning to jump just at the right time.

NET RECOVERY

Sometimes a teammate will hit the ball into the net on his or her side of the court. A player tries to recover the ball so that it will not hit the floor. If there have been one or two hits, a player can hit the ball as it bounces off the net. The player faces the net and watches it closely when the ball is going to hit. He or she uses the forearm volley to try to get the ball up high.

TEAM PLAY

Volleyball is a game in which there is a very quick shift back and forth from offense to defense. This is because the ball goes back and forth across the net quickly.

One way of scoring is that a team scores only on its own serve. This means that when a team serves and, after one or more volleys back and forth over the net, the ball lands on the other team's side, the serving team scores a point. If the ball lands on the serving team's side of the court there would be no score for the other team because it was not the serving team. Rally scoring means that a team scores a point each time it wins a volley whether it served or not.

The following are several important things to remember about offensive play.

1. The server should try to place the ball in an open space. It is also a good idea to try to serve it near the end of the court and close to the side line.
2. The ball must go over the net on the third hit. There is usually better team play when the three hits are taken.
3. A three-hit play might go as follows: the ball is received by a back-line player; his or her hit is the first one, and it goes to a front-line player; this player makes the second hit and sets it up for the teammate to spike it; and the third hit is the spike over the net. This three-hit play takes a lot of practice and teamwork.
4. It is not a good idea for the front-line players to play with their backs to the net. They should either face the net or turn the body only about halfway around.
5. Try to volley the ball high.

The following are some of the important things to remember about defensive play.

1. Always try to keep the eyes on the ball.
2. Usually try to keep one foot ahead of the other with the weight equal on both feet.
3. Most of the time a serve will be received by a back-line player. This player should volley the ball to a front-line player.
4. Sometimes if the serve is short, it can be received by a front-line player. If a player on the front line has to jump too high for the ball, he or she should let it go to a back-line player.
5. Just as in the game of baseball and softball, certain players back up other players in volleyball. The player at the right in the back line backs up the player at the right in the front line. The player in the center of the back line backs up the player in the center in the front line. The player at the left in the back line backs up the player at the left in the front line.
6. The player should call out "Mine" or "My ball" if he or she is going to take the ball. Calling out will help keep two teammates from running into each other to get the ball.

GAMES TO PRACTICE VOLLEYBALL SKILLS

It was mentioned before that there are six players on a regular volleyball team. There are three players in the front line and three players in the back line. The three players in the front line are the right forward, center forward, and left forward. The three players in the back line are the right back, center back, and left back. In the following games any number can play. In these games it is not necessary to always follow the regular rules of volleyball. The idea for these games is to learn certain skills that can help make one a better volleyball player.

Net Ball

Net Ball is played about the same as volleyball except that the ball is *thrown* back and forth across the net. The purpose is to get the players used to getting the ball over the net. If a player drops the ball, it counts a point for the other team. There can be as few as one player on a side; however, it is better to have three or more players on each side.

Keep It Up

Two or more teams of players with three or four players on a team can play this game. Each team forms a circle. On a signal, each team starts to volley the ball. The players on a team volley it to each other. They can use any kind of volley to do this. When one team allows the ball to hit the ground, it counts a point against that team.

Serve Up

Two people can play this game, or more can play is desired. The ball is served to a partner and he or she serves it back. They start out a short distance apart and then keep making the distance longer.

Volley Up

This game is the same as Serve Up except that the ball is volleyed back and forth rather than being served back and forth. A player tries to see how many good volleys he or she can make without letting the ball hit the ground.

Wall Volleyball

From two to four players can play this game. The idea of the game is to keep the ball bouncing against a wall. One player starts by serving against the wall. It is returned by the next player. Play goes on with the players taking turns hitting the ball. After the serve, the ball is volleyed against the wall. If a player allows the ball to hit the ground, the player who last hit the ball against the wall scores a point.

Volleyball Keep Away

Two teams with any number of players on a team can play this game. It is a good idea to have at least three players on a team. The team members try to volley the ball to each other. The other team tries to get the ball. If it does, the players try to volley it to each other. The team that volleys the ball the greatest number of times wins the game. This is a good game to play with a beachball.

Volleyball is one of the fastest-growing sports in the United States both in numbers of teams and participants as well as fan interest. It requires maximum teamwork and is a dynamic and interesting sport for participants and fans.

Chapter 9

CONDUCTING THE SPORTS LEARNING EXPERIENCE WITH CHILDREN

It should be obvious that the success of sports learning will depend in a large degree upon how well the experiences are presented. This is the reason for providing a detailed account of the procedure in this chapter.

The term *teacher* in the present discussion refers to any adult who will assume the responsibility for conducting sports learning experiences.

The teacher should be aware that every child is almost incredibly unique and that he or she approaches all learning tasks with his or her own level of motivation, capacity, experience and vitality. Moreover, the teacher must by a combination of emotional and logical appeal, help each individual find his or her own way through the experience and at his or her own rate. The teacher must also help the individual understand the meaning of the experience and help to incorporate it and its use into the child's own life.

The teacher's role should be that of a guide who supervises and directs desirable sports learning experiences. In providing such experiences, the teacher should constantly keep in mind how a sport can contribute to the physical, social, emotional and intellectual development of the child. This implies that the teacher should develop an understanding of the principles of learning and apply these principles properly in presenting sports learning experiences to children.

SOME PRINCIPLES OF LEARNING APPLIED TO SPORTS

There are various facts about the nature of human beings in which modern educators are more aware than educators of the past. Essentially these facts involve some of the fundamental aspects of the learning process, which all good teaching should take into account. Older ideas of teaching methods were based on the notion that the teacher was the sole authority in terms of what was best for children, and that children were expected to learn regardless of the conditions surrounding the learning situation. For the most part, modern teaching replaces the older concept with methods that are based on certain beliefs of educational psychology. Outgrowth of these beliefs emerge in the form of *principles of learning*. The following principles should provide important guidelines for adults for arranging learning experiences for children and they suggest how desirable learning can take place when the principles are satisfactorily applied to learning through sports.

1. *The child's own purposeful goals should guide learning activities*. For a desirable learning situation to prevail, adults should consider certain features about purposeful goals that guide learning activities. Of utmost importance is that the goal must seem worthwhile to the child. This will involve such factors as interest, attention and motivation. Fortunately in sports, interest, attention and motivation are likely to be "built-in" qualities. Thus, the adult does not necessarily need to "arouse" the child with various kinds of extrinsic motivating devices.

2. *The child should be given sufficient freedom to create his or her own responses in the situation faced*. This principle indicates that *problem solving* is a very important way of human learning and that the child will learn mainly through experience, either direct or indirect. This implies that an adult should provide every opportunity for the child to use judgment in the various situations that arise in the sports experience.

3. *The child agrees to and acts upon the learning that he or she considers of most value*. Children accept as most valuable those things which are of greatest interest to them. This principle implies, in part, that there should be a satisfactory balance between *needs* and *interests* of children in their sports experiences. Although it is of extreme importance to consider the

needs of children in developing experiences, an adult should keep in mind that their interest is needed if the most desirable learning is to take place.

4. *The child should be given the opportunity to share cooperatively in learning experiences with others under the guidance but not the control of the adult.* This principle is concerned with those sports experiences that involve several players. The point that should be emphasized here is that although learning is an individual matter, it can take place well in a group. This is to say that children learn individually but that socialization should be retained. This can be achieved even if there are only two members participating.

5. *The adult should act as a guide who understands the child as a growing organism.* This principle indicates that the adult should consider learning as an evolving process and not just instant behavior. If an adult is to regard his or her efforts in terms of guidance and direction of behavior that results in learning, then wisdom must be displayed as to when to "step in and teach" and when to step aside and watch for further opportunities to guide and direct behavior. The application of this principle precludes an approach that is adult dominated. In this regard the adult could be guided by the old saying "children should learn by monkeying and not by aping."

It is quite likely that adults will have good success in using the sports experiences recommended in this book if they apply the above principles. The main reason for this is that their efforts in helping children learn about sports will be in line with those conditions under which learning takes place most effectively.

CHARACTERISTICS OF GOOD TEACHERS

Over the years there have been numerous attempts to identify objectively those characteristics of good teachers that set them apart from average or poor teachers. Obviously, this is a difficult matter because of the countless variables involved.

We should keep in mind here that effective coaches are almost always also good teachers. For that reason, coaches should understand the basic principles of effective teaching.

It is entirely possible for two teachers to have the same degree of intelligence and understanding of what they are teaching. Yet, it is also possible that one of these teachers will consistently achieve good results with children, while the other will not have much success. Perhaps a good part of the reason for this difference in success lies in those individual differences of teachers that relate to certain personality factors and how they deal and interact with children. Based upon the available research and numerous interviews with both teachers and children, we have found the following characteristics tend to emerge most often among good teachers.

1. Good teachers possess those characteristics that in one way or another have a humanizing effect on children. An important factor about good teachers that appeals to most children is a sense of humor.

2. In all cases, good teachers are fair and democratic in their dealings with children and tend to maintain the same positive feelings toward the so-called "problem" child as they do with other children.

3. Another very important characteristic is that good teachers are able to relate easily to children. They have the ability and sensitivity to "listen through children's ears and see through children's eyes."

4. Good teachers are flexible. They know that different approaches need to be used with different groups of children as well as individual children. In addition, good teachers can adjust easily to changing situations.

5. Good teachers have control. Different teachers exercise control in different ways, but good teachers tend to have a minimum of control problems because they provide a learning environment where control becomes less of a problem.

TEACHING AND LEARNING IN SPORTS

The teaching-learning process is complicated and complex. For this reason it is important that teachers have as full an understanding as possible of the role of teaching and learning in sports.

Basic Considerations

The concepts of learning that a teacher subscribes to are directly related to the kind and variety of sports learning activities and experiences that he or she will provide for children. Thus, it is important for teachers to explore some of the factors that make for the most desirable and worthwhile learning. Among the factors that should help to orient the reader with regard to some basic understandings in the teaching of sports activities are (1) an understanding of the meaning of certain terms, (2) an understanding of the derivation of teaching methods, and (3) an understanding of the various learning products in sports.

Meaning of Terms

Due to the fact that certain terms, because of their multiple use, do not actually have a universal definition, no attempt will be made here to *define* terms. On the other hand, it will be the purpose of *describe* certain terms rather than attempt to define them. The reader should view descriptions of terms that follow with this general idea in mind.

Learning

Most descriptions of learning are characterized by the idea that learning involves some sort of change in the individual. This means that when an individual has learned, behavior is modified in one or more ways. Thus, a valid criterion for learning would be that after having an experience, a person could behave or perform in a way in which he or she could not have behaved or performed before having the experience.

Teaching

Several years ago the first author was addressing a group of teachers on the subject of teaching and learning. Introducing the discussion in somewhat abstract terms, he asked, "What is teaching?" After a short period of embarrassing deliberation, one member of the group interrogated the following answer with some degree of uncertainty: "Is it imparting information?" This kind of thinking is characteristic of the traditional meaning of the term teaching. A more acceptable description would be to think of it in terms of guidance, direction and supervision of behavior that results in desirable and worthwhile learning. This is to say that it is the job of the teacher to guide the child's learning rather than to impart to him or her a series of unrelated and sometimes meaningless facts.

Method

The term method might be considered as an orderly and systematic means of achieving an objective. In other words, method is concerned with "how to do" something in order to achieve desired results. If best results are to be obtained for children in their sports experiences, it becomes necessary that the most desirable sports learning experiences be provided. Consequently, it becomes essential that teachers use all of the ingenuity and resourcefulness at their command in the proper direction and guidance of these learning experiences. The procedures that teachers use are known as teaching methods and in the case of coaching, coaching methods.

Derivation of Teaching Methods

Beginning teachers often ask, "Where do we get our ideas for teaching methods?" For the most part this question should be considered in general terms. Although there are a variety of acceptable teaching procedures, all of these are likely to be derived from two somewhat broad sources.

The first of these involves an accumulation of knowledge of educational psychology and what is known about the learning process in providing for sports learning experiences. The other is the practices of successful teachers.

In most instances, professional preparation of prospective teachers includes at least some study of educational psychology as it applies to the learning process and certain accepted principles of learning. With this basic information it is expected that beginning teachers have sufficient knowledge to make application of it in the practical situation.

It has been our observation over a period of years that many beginning teachers tend to rely too much upon the practices of successful teachers as a source of teaching methods. The validity of this procedure is based on the assumption that such successful practices are likely to have as their bases the application of fundamental psychological principles of learning. Nevertheless, it should be the responsibility of every teacher or coach to become familiar with the basic psychological principles of learning and to attempt to apply these in the best possible way when providing the most desirable and worthwhile learning experiences for children.

Learning Products in Sports

In general, three learning products can be identified that accrue from participation in sports activities, namely, *direct*, *incidental*, and *indirect*. In a well-planned teaching/coaching program, these learning products should develop satisfactorily through sports activities.

Direct learning products are those that are the direct object of teaching. For instance, running, dribbling, dodging, passing and catching are some of the important skills necessary for reasonable degrees of proficiency in the game of basketball. Through the learning of skills, more enjoyment is derived from participating in an activity than just the practice of the skills. For this reason, the learning of skills is one of the primary direct objects of sports teaching. However, it should be understood that certain incidental and indirect learning products can result from direct teaching in sports. The zeal of a participant to become a more proficient performer gives rise to certain incidental learning products. These may be inherent in the realization and acceptance of practices of healthful living, which make the individual a more skilled performer in the activity.

Attitudes have often been considered in terms of behavior tendencies and as such might well be concerned with indirect learning products. This type of learning product involves such qualities as sportsmanship, appreciation of certain aspects of the activity and other factors that involve the adjustment and modification of the individual's reaction to others.

Adults who have the responsibility for providing sports programs for children should give a great deal of consideration to these various kinds of learning products. This is particularly important if children are to receive the full benefit of sports learning experiences that are provided for them.

PHASES OF THE TEACHING-LEARNING SITUATION

There are certain fundamental phases involved in almost every sports teaching-learning situation. These are (1) auditory input, (2) visual input, (3) participation and (4) evaluation. Although these four phases are likely to be weighted in various degrees, they will occur in the teaching of practically every sports situation regardless of the type of activity that is being taught. While the application of the various phases may be of a general nature, they nevertheless should be utilized in such a way that they become specific in a particular situation. Depending upon the type of activity, the use and application of the various phases should always include flexibility and awareness of the objectives of the specific teaching/coaching situation.

Auditory-Input Phase

The term *auditory* may be described as stimulation occurring through the organs of hearing. The term *input* is concerned with the use of as many media as are deemed necessary for a particular teaching-learning situation. The term *output* is concerned with behaviors or reactions of the learner resulting from the various forms of input. Auditory input involves the various learning media that are directed to the auditory sense. This should not be interpreted to mean that the auditory-input phase is a one-way process. While much of such input may originate with the teacher, consideration should also be given to the verbal interaction among children and between children and the teacher.

Sports provide a most desirable opportunity for learning through direct, purposeful experience. In other words, the sports learning situation is "learning by doing," or learning through pleasurable physical activity. Although verbalization might well be kept to a minimum, a certain amount of auditory input, which provides for auditory association, appears to be essential for a satisfactory teaching-learning situation. The quality of "kinesthetic feel" may be described as the process of changing ideas into muscular action and is of primary importance in the proper acquisition of sports skills. It might be said that the auditory-input phase helps to set the stage for a kinesthetic concept (muscular action) of the particular activity being taught.

Great care should be taken with the auditory-input phase in sports teaching-learning situations. The ensuing discussions are intended to suggest to the reader ways in which the greatest benefits can accrue when using this particular learning medium.

Preparing Children for Listening

Since it is likely that the initial part of the auditory-input phase will originate with the teacher, care should be taken to prepare children for listening. The teacher may set the scene for listening by relating the activity to the interests of children. In addition, the teacher should be on the alert to help children develop their own purposes for listening.

In preparing children to listen, the teacher should be aware that it is of importance that the comfort of children be taken into consideration and that attempts should be made for removing any possible attention-distracting factors. Although evidence concerning the effect of environmental distractions on listening effectiveness is not in great abundance, there is reason to believe that distraction does interfere with listening comprehension. Moreover, it is well known that being able to see as well as hear the speaker is an important factor in listening distraction.

These factors have a variety of implications for the auditory-input phase. For example, consideration should be given to the placement of children when a sports activity requires auditory input by the teacher. This means, for instance, that if the teacher is providing auditory input from a circle formation, the teacher should take a position as part of the circle instead of speaking from the center of the circle. Also, it might be well for teachers to consider that an object, such as a ball, can become an attention-distracting factor when an activity is being discussed. The attention of the children is sometimes focused on the ball, and they may not listen to what is being said. The teacher might wish to place such an object out of the line of vision until time for its use is most appropriate.

Teacher-Child and Child-Child Interaction

It was mentioned previously that the auditory-input phase is a two-way process. As such, it is important to take into account certain factors involving verbal interaction of children with children, and teacher with children.

By "democracy" some people seem to mean everyone doing or saying whatever happens to cross his or her mind at the moment. This raises the question of control, and it should be emphasized that group discussions, if they are to be democratic, must be in control. This is to say that if a group discussion is to succeed it must be under control, so let us stress that democracy implies discipline and control.

Group discussion is a kind of sociointellectual exercise (which can involve numerous bodily movements, of course) just as a sports activity is a kind of sociointellectual exercise (which can involve higher mental functioning). Both imply individual discipline to keep play moving within bounds, and both require moderators (officials) overseeing, though not participating in, the play in the manner that is objective and transcendent from the heat of competition. In brief, disciplined, controlled group discussion can be a training ground for living in a society in which both individual and group interests are profoundly respected – just as sports can serve a comparable function.

Another important function in teacher-child interaction is with the time given to questions after the teacher has provided auditory-input. The teacher should give time for questions but should be very skillful in the use of questions. It must be determined immediately whether or not a question is a legitimate one. This implies that the type of questions asked can help serve as criteria for the teacher to evaluate the auditory-input phase. For example, if numerous questions are asked, it is apparent that either the auditory input from the teacher was unsatisfactory, or the children were not paying attention.

Directionality of Sound

Summarizing recent findings concerned with the directionality of sound, a number of interesting factors important to the auditory-input phase have emerged. For example, individuals tend to initiate movements toward the direction from which the sound emanates. That is, if a verbal clue is given that instructs the individual to move a body segment or segments to the left, but the verbal clue emanates from the right side of the individual, the initial motor response is to the right, followed by a reverse response to the left. It is recommended that when working on direction of motor responses with children, one should make certain that the sound cues come from the direction in which the motor response is made. The point is that children have enough difficulty in discriminating left from right without confusing them further.

Visual-Input Phase

Various estimates indicate that the visual sense brings us approximately three-fourths of our knowledge. If this postulation can be used as a valid criterion, the merits of the visual-input phase in teaching about sports are readily discernible. In many cases, visual input, which should provide for visual-motor association, serves as a happy medium between verbal symbols and direct participation in helping teachers further prepare children for the kinesthetic feel mentioned previously.

In general, there are two types of visual input which can be used satisfactorily in teaching about sports. These are visual symbols and human demonstration (live performance).

Visual Symbols

Included among the visual symbols used in sports are motion pictures and various kinds of flat or still pictures. One of the disadvantages of the latter centers around the difficulty of portraying movement with a still figure. Although movement is obtained with a motion picture, it is not depicted in third dimension, which causes some degree of ineffectiveness when this medium is used. One valuable use of visual symbols is that of employing diagrams to show the dimension of activity areas. Computer screens can of course also depict movement with effective motion, color and in some cases a sense of dimension.

Human Demonstration

Some of the guides to action in the use of demonstration follow:

1. If the teacher plans to demonstrate, this should be included in the preparation by practicing and rehearsing the demonstration.
2. The teacher does not need to do all of the demonstrating; in fact, in some cases it may be much more effective to have one or more children demonstrate. Since the teacher might be expected to be a skilled performer, a demonstration by a child will oftentimes serve to show other children that one of their peers can perform the activity and that they should be able to do it also.
3. A demonstration should be based on the skill and ability of a given group of children. If it appears to be too difficult for them, they might not want to attempt the activity.
4. When at all possible, a demonstration should parallel the timing and the conditions under which it will be put to practical application. However, if the situation is one in which the movements are complex or done with great speed, it might be well to have the demonstration conducted at a slower rate than that involved in the actual performance situation.
5. If there is a group the children should be arranged so that everyone is in a favorable position to see the demonstration. Moreover, the children should be able to view the demonstration from a position where it takes place. For example, if the activity is to be performed in a lateral plane, children should be placed so that they can see it from this position.
6. Although auditory input and human demonstration can be satisfactorily combined in many situations, care should be taken that auditory input is not lost, because the visual sense offsets the auditory sense. That is, one should not become an attention-distracting factor for the other. It will be up to the teacher to determine the amount of verbalization that should accompany the demonstration.
7. After the demonstration has been presented it might be a good practice to demonstrate again and have the children go through the movements with the demonstrator. This provides for the use of the kinesthetic sense together with the visual sense that makes for close integration of the two sensory stimuli.

Participation Phase

The following considerations should be kept in mind in connection with the participation phase of teaching.

1. The practice session should be planned so that the greatest possible amount of time is given to participation.
2. If the activity does not progress as expected in the participation phase, perhaps the fault may lie in the procedures used in the auditory-input and visual-input phases. Participation then becomes a criterion for the evaluation of former phases.
3. The teacher should take into account the fact that the original attempts in learning an activity should meet with a reasonable degree of success.
4. The teacher should constantly be aware of the possibility of fatigue of children during participation and should understand that individual differences of children create a variation with regard to how rapidly fatigue takes place.
5. Participation should be worthwhile for every child, and all children should have the opportunity to achieve.
6. During the participation phase the teacher should constantly analyze the performance of children in order to determine those who need improvement in skills. Behaviorisms of children should be observed while they are engaging in the sports activity. For example, various types of emotional behavior might be noted in sports situations that might not be indicated in any other experience.
7. Problems involved during the participation should be kept in mind for subsequent evaluation with the children.

Evaluation Phase

Evaluation is a very important phase of the sports teaching-learning situation, and yet, perhaps one of the most neglected aspects of it. For instance, it is not an uncommon procedure to have a practice session end without an evaluation of the results of the session.

Children should be given the opportunity to discuss the session and to suggest ways in which improvement might be effected. When this procedure is followed, children are placed in a problem-solving situation and desirable learning is more likely, with the teacher guiding learning rather than dominating the situation in a direction-giving type of procedure. Also more and better continuity is likely to be provided from one session to another when time is taken for evaluation; in addition, children are much more likely to develop a clearer understanding of the purpose of sports if they are given an opportunity to discuss the procedures involved.

Ordinarily, the evaluation phase should take place at the end of the session. Experience has shown that a satisfactory evaluation procedure can be effected in five to six minutes, depending upon the nature of the activity and upon what actually occurred during the session. Under certain circumstances, if an activity is not proceeding well in the participation phase, it may be desirable to stop and carry out what is known as a "spot" evaluation. This does not mean that the teacher should stop an activity every time the situation is not developing according to plan. A suggestion or hint to children who are having difficulty with performance can perhaps preclude the need for having all of the children cease participation. On the other hand, if the situation is such that the needs of the group will best be met by a discussion concerning the solution of a problem, the teacher is indeed justified in stopping the activity and conducting an evaluation "on the spot."

In concluding this chapter, let us say that if the teacher is to provide sports learning experiences that contribute to total development of children, there must be a clear perspective of the total learning that is expected from the area of sports. This implies that in order to provide for progression in sports learning there must be some means of preserving continuity from one session to another. Consequently, each individual session becomes a link in the chain of sports learnings that contribute to the total development of the child. Experience has shown that the implementation of this theory into reality can be most successfully accomplished by wise and careful planning of every session.

INDEX